A PIECE OF MY SOUL

A PIECE OF MY SOUL

QUILTS BY BLACK ARKANSANS

CUESTA BENBERRY

WITH AN INTRODUCTION BY RAYMOND G. DOBARD

The University of Arkansas Press
Fayetteville
2000

Copyright © 2000 by The University of Arkansas Press

All rights reserved
Manufactured in Korea
04   03   02   01   00   5   4   3   2   1

Designed by Liz Lester

⊛   The paper used in this publication meets the minimum requirements of the American
National Standard for Permanence of Paper for Printed Library Materials Z39.48-1984.

LIBRARY OF CONGRESS CATALOGING-IN-PUBLICATION DATA

Benberry, Cuesta.
    A piece of my soul : quilts by black Arkansans / Cuesta Benberry ; with an
introduction by Raymond G. Dobard.
        p.   cm.
    Includes bibliographical references (p.   ) and index.
    ISBN 1-55728-620-5 (cloth : alk. paper)
    1. Afro-American quilts—Arkansas—Themes, motives. 2. Afro-American
quiltmakers—Arkansas—Biography. I. Title.
NK9112 .B457   2000
746.46'08996'0730767—dc21   00-009638

Acknowledgments

I must first pay homage to the black quiltmakers of Arkansas whose works are displayed in this exhibition. During my initial visit to the Old State House Museum, as each quilt was unfolded, I felt surprise, awe, incredulity, happiness, for indeed these quilts touched my soul. The staff, of course, wanted me to see as many of the quilts as possible, but I delayed the viewing process somewhat because I wanted to linger over each quilt. I will never forget the Hattie Collins Log Cabin quilt with its soft muted colors. It spoke to me in a way that few quilts have. I fell in love with all of the wonderful quilts and regret I never met any of the quiltmakers, most of whom are now deceased.

I am deeply indebted to Bill Gatewood, Ronnie Nichols, Larry Ahart, and all the museum staff for their encouragement and their sharing of vital information about Arkansas and the history of its black population from an Arkansas insider's viewpoint, much not available to me, an outsider, when consulting the usual resources. Gail Moore has been an absolute joy with whom to work. She has gone above and beyond her duties to assist me in securing all materials needed, provided illuminating counsel, and has been unbelievably patient. My erudite editor, Georgeanne Sisco, has the rare ability to make difficult work seem painless. I was amazed, but joyful when I was made an honorary "Arkansas Traveler."

Of immense help to me were the field notes quilt historian Dr. Sandra Todaro, Shreveport, Louisiana, provided for the Old State House Museum when she personally interviewed many of the black Arkansas quilters and their descendants who had moved to Louisiana. As I was unable to interview the quilters, Sandra Todaro's fulsome field notes were critical in some instances and allowed me to see the quilters "through the eyes" of an experienced recorder of the history of quilts and their makers.

I thank Dr. Raymond Dobard for his introduction with its insightful analysis of the text. His valuable essay reveals the rare combination of both scholarly and practical knowledge of quilts that he possesses.

To Deborah Harding, I must express my sincere thanks. At a critial juncture during the writing of this book, Deborah Harding's generous contributions assured the book's completion.

For their encouragement and their skilled editing, I am happy to have had the opportunity to work with Kevin Brock, Abigail Smith, Deborah Self, Brian King, and Lawrence Malley, director of the University of Arkansas Press. The entire Arkansas experience has been a memorable one.

Contents

Preface

In 1989, when invited to lecture on African American quilt history, I visited for the first time the Old State House Museum in Little Rock, Arkansas. At the same time the Old State House Museum was hosting a national traveling exhibition of African American quilts. Hung in a spacious front gallery of the museum, the visiting quilts presented a spectacular picture—a mélange of the most vivid colors. As the quilts were pieced in a free-form, improvisational manner, the juxtaposition of the brilliant blues, bold reds, and bright yellows had a closer affinity to modern abstract art than to the precision-oriented traditional American patchwork quilt. While acknowledging the electrifying visual impact of the traveling quilts, I, as a researcher of quilt history, began to probe for more information. Where were the quilts made? When were they made, and did the dates of the fabrics in the quilts confirm the dates delegated to them? Had the quilt designs been assigned a specific name? Were the quiltmakers identified as to name, birthplace, and age? By reading the captions affixed to the gallery walls, I learned that the majority of the quilts had been made in southern regions of the country by persons who had been born and reared in the South. Most of the quilts were of recent vintage, having been constructed circa 1970 to the 1980s.

In a smaller adjoining gallery an entirely diffferent group of quilts was on display. The museum curator announced, "These are our local quilts. All of them were made by black Arkansans." In stark contrast to the traveling exhibit quilts in the larger gallery, the Arkansas black-made quilts were characterized by subdued, soft colorations and had been, for the most part, fashioned in recognizable traditional quilt patterns. Some of the Arkansas quilts were quite old and predated the visiting quilts by many years. Obviously made as utilitarian bedcovers, the Arkansas quilts showed signs of use, and their gentle colors could perhaps be attributed as much to launderings as to age. Yet they were not threadbare, nor did they show significant fading, an indication the quilts had been cherished and given care. The Old State House

Museum curator said the museum was continuing to acquire black Arkansans' quilts, and planned to build a sizeable collection of their textile works.

With those two groups of quilts, side by side in adjoining galleries, the visiting quilts and the black Arkansans' ones, the dissimilarities were strikingly apparent. No better example of the diversity that exists in black-made quilts could be found. Despite a widely accepted notion that black quiltmakers' works displayed a single aesthetic orientation based on unconscious cultural memories of their African homeland, these two groups of black-made quilts illustrated the immense diversity that is the hallmark of African American quiltmaking. I vowed that someday I would return to the Old State House Museum and fully examine and study their collection of African American quilts. Although at that time it was a relatively small collection, I had never encountered such a rich source of African American quilt history in all of the years I had pursued the investigations. Meanwhile, the Old State House Museum continued its quest to obtain more black Arkansans' quilts to achieve its ultimate goal, which was to mount an exhibition of the quilts to honor a heretofore largely ignored segment of the state's population, the African American quiltmakers of Arkansas.

By 1997 the Old State House Museum's collection numbered more than eighty quilts, and I was invited to curate its proposed exhibition: *A Piece of My Soul: Quilts by Black Arkansans.* Remembering the museum's appealing quilts I had seen in 1989, I wondered if the new additions to the collection would be equally as captivating. When the Old State House Museum staff persons Gail Moore and Georgeanne Sisco unrolled the quilts on a long table, I was not disappointed. Instead I stood transfixed, awed by the diversity of designs unfurled. Now the collection included quilts similar in construction to the traveling exhibit quilts of 1989: improvisationally pieced quilts, novelty quilts, original designs, traditional quilts, antique quilts, recently made quilts, a huge variety, all made by black Arkansans. We measured and turned the quilts, peered though magnifying glasses at the threads and stitches, matched pattern names, dated the fabrics, photographed the quilts, traced the families represented, pored over documents, all of the usual processes needed, but there was more: my personal responses to these exceptional quilts are recorded here in *A Piece of My Soul: Quilts by Black Arkansans.*

Introduction

A Patchwork of People and Patterns

*The [Arkansas] black experience is varied, complex, some-
times tragic, sometimes joyous, and often at the heart of the
American dream.*

—Tom Baskett Jr.,
*Persistence of the Spirit:
The Black Experience in Arkansas, 1986*

A Piece of My Soul is an American patchwork of quilts and biogra-
phies skillfully pieced together by Cuesta Benberry into an exceptional
exhibit and thought-provoking catalog. Through juxtaposing genealogical information, migration documentation, family histories, quilt patterns and styles, Benberry makes it possible for the black quilters of
Arkansas to share pieces of their souls with all who see the exhibition
and read this catalog. Variety enlivens this exhibition and proves that no
one style of quilt is privileged as the quintessential African American
Arkansas model. Similar to African American quilts in other states, the
Arkansas works are unique and intimate to the individuals who made
them. The quilts in *A Piece of My Soul* range in age, materials used, construction methods, aesthetic choices, and gender of the makers. In style,
everything from whole-cloth quilts through medallion, appliqué, geometric piecing, and crazy quilts to the well-known but misunderstood
utilitarian quilt are all represented. The visual vocabulary of the Arkansas
black quilters is impressive, and the syntax is striking. From the three-
dimensional Pine Cone quilt of Oscar Evans to the "fool the eye" Four
Patch of Leonia Taylor, optical illusions prevail.

The exhibit also includes works with traditional pattern names such
as Log Cabin, Double Wedding Ring, Dresden Plate, Grandmother's
Flower Garden, Jacob's Ladder, and Sunbonnet Sue. What is intriguing is how these patterns are pieced, employing color schemes that
impart distinction. Whether inventive or traditional, the quilts afford

us the rare opportunity to see works from several generations within one family. We are able to see what techniques and color choices are inherited and which are original to the quilter. This quilt lineage becomes important when attempting to trace color combinations, stitching techniques, and patterns which modern scholarship links to special quilts used on the Underground Railroad. We might ask ourselves if familiarity has obscured something that was once very important. Are pieces of the soul flashes of memory, of the way grandma or great-grandma made quilts? Can family heritage include using quilts to convey messages?

What about the colors? Blue and white was a popular combination in mid-nineteenth-century quilts. So too was red and white. And yet we cannot dismiss the African use of these colors in which blue and white is a protective combination for the Ibo and the Yoruba of Nigeria. Red and white are the colors of the Yoruba god of thunder, Shango; red and black are associated with Eshu, the guardian of the crossroads. Are color preferences handed down from one generation to the next rooted in early nineteenth-century African traditions? If so, these African retentions are the product of quilting in the manner of grandma or great-grandma, and not the product of "genetic" memory. When we read about Hattie Jones, her *Brick Quilt,* and her belief in evil spirits, are we possibly reading about one woman's response to what Robert Farris Thompson identifies as an African belief from Senegambia that evil travels in straight lines? Does Hattie stagger the fabric bricks in her quilt to thwart the path of evil? Is Hattie Jones sewing protection in the form of a quilt? Are other black Arkansas quilters doing more than celebrating color and texture?

The quilts of the Shed-Bennett family of Camden are highlighted as pieces of a family's soul, with Asia Cummings Shed as the matriarch of a tradition of fine needlework. While Asia's star quilts dazzle the viewer, her Lily quilt of circa 1890–1910 is puzzling. Is there particular meaning to the roman cross and the zigzag or streak-of-lightning designs in this Lily quilt? Is it coincidental that the cross and the zigzag are reminiscent of the Bakongo cosmogram, with the zigzag design reading as Kalunga, a stylized stream of water beneath which is the world of the spirit? The Lily pattern is native to the Carolinas, not to Arkansas. Was this quilt treasured by Asia, as Benberry notes, because it was a fancy or show quilt which Asia reserved for special occasions? Asia was not the only Shed-Bennett family member to produce quilts that might bear special meaning. Malsie Shed-Bennett was another.

According to Benberry, the Log Cabin quilt of circa 1930–50 is mysterious because of the meticulous piecing of solid dark sections placed at the top of the quilt. Is there any possible tie between the use of dark fabric on Malsie's Log Cabin quilt and the theory of some quilt researchers that the use of black fabric was part of a signaling system on the Underground Railroad? It appears that the family has some particular knowledge. Malsie pieced another quilt, a *Trip Around the World,* which is possibly tied to the Underground Railroad activity in the Carolinas. In the book titled *Hidden in Plain View: A Secret Story of Quilts and the Underground Railroad,* written by Jacqueline Tobin and Raymond G. Dobard, the Log Cabin pattern as well as Stars and Trip Around the World are cited in an Underground Railroad quilt code from Charleston, South Carolina. Is there a connection here between the Shed-Bennett family and coded quilts? Further investigation of the Shed-Bennett family and their quiltmaking traditions might produce some startling facts.

When researching African American quilts in a state such as Arkansas where a people of color lived since the eighteenth century, it is wise to keep an open and inquiring mind. In traditional Benberry fashion, a wealth of material is placed before us to analyze and to formulate theories. The family histories with their detailed genealogies provide an excellent point of departure for any researcher seeking to fully understand the inspiration behind the quilts of the Arkansas black community. Refreshing and ingenious quilt designs are visual connections to the past and to the complexity of nineteenth- and early twentieth-century life in America.

Both the pragmatic and the esoteric become ties for the African American quilt, a quilt that often contains a surprise in the batting. As Benberry informs us, many old quilts serve as batting for the quilts of the next generation. This apparently practical use of an old quilt is also a means of cherishing the handiwork of an ancestor and of ensuring a tangible connection. One would not throw away a tattered quilt which grandma made, especially if grandma has passed away. Tying the quilt instead of stitching it affords the next generation quilter the opportunity of metaphorically as well as ritually bonding with the previous. The concept of "connections" is important to the African American sensibility and vital to heritage.

The very act of tying the quilt might also have roots in African traditions in which tying knots for the Bakongo people of West Africa is integral to the making of a Nkisi, an object empowered to protect. The act of tying becomes a personal ritual for the Arkansas quilters. On a practical level, tying is the chosen technique if the batting is composed of heavy material. On a personal level, tying may be a ritual act, one of reverence and of the desire to maintain a connection with a loved one. In this way the quilt is a personal icon for the quilter, one in which she/he can wrap one's self and feel a communion with the deceased.

Jessie Jones of Monticello, Arkansas, tied many of her quilts. We learn about her quilting methods and preferred quilt style thanks to Benberry's thorough documentation. According to Benberry, Jessie Jones was very fond of the strip-quilt style. The strip quilt is a staple among African American utilitarian quilts because of its practical use of fabric remnants and its possible continuation of an African textile tradition.

The strip quilt and its first cousin the string quilt are made by sewing small scraps of fabric together, forming one vertical "strip" of cloth. Frequently, the fabric remnants were attached to a newspaper template. When a newspaper-backed strip is covered with fabric, the excess bits of fabric are trimmed away, leaving a clean vertical strip ready to be joined lengthwise to another. This process of producing strips of multicolored fabric joined lengthwise to fashion one cloth is reminiscent of Kente cloth weaving in Ghana, West Africa. Simplicity in quilt-top construction and employing an economy of means demonstrated by the use of newspaper are as much a part of the African American quilt heritage as the strip-woven cloths of Africa. In fact, newspaper templates were used extensively.

When researchers find a quilt top which has been constructed using the newspaper template method, they carefully examine the back of the quilt top, hoping to find bits of newspaper still attached to the fabric. The newspaper fragments might contain clues to help date the quilt. Clues lay hidden in bits of advertisement or in photo scraps of items for sale. Old mail-order catalogs such as the Sears and Roebuck circa 1909, or "wish books" as they were sometimes called, help to identify and to date the articles advertised in the newspaper fragments. Sometimes a fragment of paper with an actual date printed on it is found. It is not unusual to find African American quilts with the newspaper still attached to the fabric because newspaper was also used as inexpensive batting. If we carefully examine the early twentieth-century quilts in this exhibit of Arkansas quilts, we will probably find examples of newspaper template use. While the use of newspaper for templates as well as for batting is not original to African American quilters, newspaper was a popular template material for black quilters, especially in the rural South.

Once all paper-pieced strips of fabric, geometric blocks, or free-cut fabric shapes are sewn together to make the quilt top, the top is then layered on to the batting and the backing, basted together, and either tied or stitched. Often the knots used to secure the beginning and the end of a row of quilting stitches are left on the surface and not pulled in between the quilt top and the batting. These knots either add to the rustic charm of the quilt or are considered an eyesore, depending on the aesthetic taste and/or knowledge of the viewer. Researchers continue to question the knots and the large stitches. Are they the product of practicality or vestiges of some earlier style?

I believe that these so-called awkward stitches and large knots were once part of a mapping vocabulary for quilts used on the Underground Railroad. In the book *Hidden in Plain View,* we read the words of Mrs. Ozella McDaniel Williams of Charleston, South Carolina. According to Mrs. Williams, the stitching and the knots formed a "language" for escaping slaves. (For further information regarding the use of knots in quilt codes, see *Hidden in Plain View,* pages 71, 72, 81.) I suspect that the stitching-knots, the uneven or large visible stitches and quilt patterns worked in tandem to indicate landmarks, milage, and safe dwelling places. The large knots left visible on the quilt top and/or backing are distinct from those found in quilt ties. Envision a utilitarian quilt top composed of rectangles, squares, irregular shapes and some geometric patterns, all in earth tone colors with some of the fabric stripped, textured and/or printed. Might such a composition simulate furrowed land, fields of different crops, ponds, streams, woodlands, particular trees, distinctive rock formations, hills, and other landmarks? Might not a zigzag motif read as a major river? Would we not have the visual elements needed for creating a topographical map in the guise of a quilt? Sometimes the simplest compositions are the most informative.

Even simple appliqué floral designs can be intriguing. A case in point is the floral appliqué quilt of Alice Trammell, a former slave from Magnolia. Benberry introduces the mystery surrounding Alice's unusual floral motif and its connection to slavery in the Carolinas. She questions Alice's motive for making the quilt and raises other fascinating questions. Is it possible that this floral design is one of the several patterns now being considered as part of a visual communication system that operated on the Underground Railroad? What about some of the other black Arkansans' quilts exhibited in *A Piece of My Soul?*

Not every quilt will be stitched in mystery or laden with covert messages. Many of the quilts exhibited here are the product of creative minds and joy-filled souls. By documenting these quilts in a journalistic manner, Benberry clearly articulates the story behind each quilt and quiltmaker without any bias or embellishment. This exhibition and catalog are in the finest Benberry tradition. We are all invited to see the quilts for the material culture that they are and to be inspired. The viewer/reader is left to interpret and to theorize, bringing to the exhibit ideas that will either be confirmed or refuted. We are thankful for these radiant glimpses into some very rich souls.

—Raymond G. Dobard

Tracing the Line

Blacks in Arkansas: A Brief Historical Overview

From the earliest record, the history of Arkansas has been inextricably intertwined with the history of its black residents. Blacks lived in Arkansas long before President Thomas Jefferson acquired the district of Arkansas in the Louisiana Purchase of 1803. According to historian Louise Gordon, slavery was introduced into French Arkansas in 1686 by the French explorer Henri de Tonti.[1] Historical records indicate that although a greater proportion of the black population in Arkansas during the antebellum period was enslaved, there were free blacks living in the district. By the time Arkansas was admitted to the Union as a slave state in 1836, blacks had lived in the region for over one hundred years.

> The real history of black Arkansans . . . Rather than one black experience there have been many. Rather than simply *existing* in conditions beyond their control, black people have dealt with their world and helped to shape it. Working against heavy odds, they have made places for themselves in the Arkansas story . . . the [Arkansas] black experience is varied, complex, sometimes tragic, sometimes joyous, and often at the heart of the American dream.[2]

An experience of black Arkansans is currently being explored by examining and relating the history of one of their material culture artifacts, the patchwork quilt.

A distinctive feature of the late twentieth century's national quilt revival was the unprecedented attention paid to African American quilts and quilters. Heretofore, black made quilts had been virtually ignored in annals of American patchwork quilts. Beginning in the last quarter of the twentieth century, comprehensive investigations of African American quilts on a national scale were initiated. Gradually research-based essays, periodical articles, books, and museum catalogs devoted, wholly or partially, to African American quilts were published. Within

Arkansas Centennial

the state of Arkansas, the quiltmaking contributions of its black citizens were acknowledged as significant.

The Rogers Historical Museum in Rogers, Arkansas, cited a group of black women in Fayetteville, Arkansas, who in the 1920s formed a club known as The Modern Priscillas.[3] While the club was not specifically formed as a quilting organization, it was a social club, whose members did sew and make quilts. Their bedcovers were quilted communally during their weekly meetings at the members' homes. Widespread publicity was accorded to an Arkansas black quilt cottage industry formed by two sisters, Graffie Jackson and Jean Johnson. Based in Lexa, Arkansas, the sisters started the quilt organization, Arkansas Country Quilts, in 1986. With the assistance of the Arkansas Industrial Development Commission, they were able to expand their building and the number of quiltmakers needed to make the quilts.[4] While conducting his nationwide survey of African American quilters, Roland Freeman interviewed and photographed quilters in Hope, Forrest City, and Hot Springs, Arkansas. Perhaps the most extraordinary of black Arkansan quilting family configurations Roland Freeman discovered consisted of a mother, daughter, and the daughter's husband, all practicing quiltmakers, the Hale family of Hot Springs.[5]

Arkansas Crossroads

Arkansas's Black Emigrants' Quilts

To place the topic of the investigations of black Arkansans' quilts in a historical context, it should be noted the majority of the collectors and researchers pursued their studies of African American quilts outside the state of Arkansas. And so, some of the first documented quilts of black Arkansans were found in places other than the areas of their original creation. Arkansas-made quilts were discovered in Arizona, California, Oregon, Ohio, Michigan, and also in contiguous states such as Louisiana and Texas. Reflected in this far-flung placement of Arkansas quilts were the migratory patterns of Arkansas's black families who left the state at various times. An especially large influx of black Arkansans into other states appears to have occurred in the 1940s, during and after World War II, as they sought better job opportunities. Their homemade bedcovers accompanied the families' relocations.

A 1981 quilt exhibition *Geometry in Motion: Afro-American Quiltmakers in Pinal County, Arizona,* produced by James S. Griffith, Arizona State University Folklore Arts coordinator, had a sizeable number of quilts in it that had been created in southwest Arkansas.[6] Continued research by James Griffith of the quilt collections of former southwest Arkansas residents revealed a startling anomaly. He found many quilts with a black-and-white coloration. The quilt-top patterns were unlike, but there was the same two-color black-and-white color scheme on each quilt. He planned to investigate whether black-and-white quilts were idiosyncratic to southwestern Arkansas quiltmakers.

Quilts of black Arkansans were found in Michigan, a favored destination of migrating Arkansas black families. When the Michigan Quilt Project led by director Marsha MacDowell conducted its 1984–1986 statewide quilt survey, black-made quilts originally from Arkansas were among the quilts documented. Noted was a wedding gift quilt in the Snail's Trail pattern pieced in 1937 by the Missionary Society of the Hughes Missionary Baptist Church, Hughes, Arkansas, for one of its members who now resides in Muskegon, Michigan.[7] Entered into the survey record was an original quilt designed by a mother-daughter team in Magnolia, Arkansas, circa 1900. Their quilt was pieced from bleached and home-dyed, hog-feed sacks.[8] An unusual floral appliqué quilt made in 1912 by a former slave, Alice Trammell of Magnolia, Arkansas, generated much interest among investigators of African American quilt history.[9] That quilt design had been the object of years of search for its place of origin. Not until the South Carolina and North Carolina quilt documentation projects were conducted was it confirmed the quilt design was indigenous to the southeastern coastal regions of the United States. It appeared time and again in the quilt search projects of those areas, but was seldom found in other parts of the United States. Finding an example of this rare design made by a former slave from Magnolia, Arkansas, added another dimension to the mystery and presented more questions to ponder. Where did Alice Trammell obtain this mid-nineteenth-century quilt design? As she made the quilt approximately forty years after slavery ended, when did she acquire the pattern? Did she have any Carolina connections? Was her quilt found in Michigan the sole example of this design she ever made? Gladys-Marie Fry, a researcher of slave-made quilts, interviewed the quiltmaker's granddaughter and learned much about Alice Trammell's life in Magnolia.[10]

Quite a few Arkansas black-made quilts have been unearthed in California by Eli Leon, a collector of African American quilts. A very striking Double Wedding Ring quilt in his collection was made in Sweet Home, Arkansas, by Emma Hall, circa 1940.[11] Other quilts in his collection came from Arkansas locations such as Gould, Pine Bluff, Tulip, Prescott, Paraloma, and Ozan.

A large percentage of the Old State House Museum's quilt collection came from black Arkansans who emigrated to Louisiana. Black families of southern Arkansas who barely managed to eke out a living as sharecropper farmers moved across the border into northern Louisiana. Attracted by the prospect of obtaining work in the area's lumber industry sawmills, these Arkansas families seeking relief from severe poverty made the difficult decision to relocate. Their quilts were packed as part of their household belongings. Over time some of the black families moved still farther south into Louisiana, even as far as the New Orleans area.

> For many black and white farmers, the Depression years meant the end of a way of life. They either sold out, lost their land and became renters or sharecroppers, or moved to the city. A significant number of black landowners with small, inherited farms managed to hang on; but for sharecroppers, black and white, life continued to be tough.[12]

Years later when the quilt revival was sweeping the nation, and various dealers, collectors, and researchers traveled to the South in search of African American quilts, the first most common reaction of the southern black quilt owners, sometimes two or three generations removed from the original Arkansas quiltmakers, was complete surprise. Their quilts had usually been given to family members, to other relatives, to friends, to neighbors who experienced disasters, always donated for warm bedcovers. Why would anyone want to buy old, sometimes even ragged quilts? Before much time had passed, however, these black people realized it was possible to sell their old quilts.

Meanwhile, back in Little Rock, the Old State House Museum and the Arkansas Territorial Restoration were committed to researching and reclaiming the material culture of Arkansas. One of the Old State House Museum's on-going projects was to build a representative collection of quilts made by black Arkansans. There was a small quilt collection in place, but the museum wished to enlarge it. Concurrent with the Arkansas museum's effort, quilt historian Sandra Todaro inaugurated a statewide quilt survey across the border, the Louisiana Quilt Project. Various quilts, several black-made, brought to sites of "Quilt Days" to be documented as Louisiana quilts were actually Arkansas quilts. Just by happenstance, one day Sandra Todaro was talking with a friend who was on the staff of the Old State House Museum. She told Sandra about the museum's current project. Some of the former black Arkansans had indicated at the time their quilts were being recorded in the Louisiana survey, they were contemplating selling their quilts, but the Louisiana Quilt Project's policy excluded the buying or selling of any quilts brought in for documentation. Sandra Todaro then put the black quilt owners in touch with the Old State House Museum. The former Arkansas residents were overjoyed at the possibility their quilts would be placed in a museum in their home state. Although preoccupied with the Louisiana Quilt Project, Sandra was enthusiastic about the Old State House Museum's undertaking. She knew other black Arkansas quilters living in Louisiana who had never brought their quilts to the Louisiana Quilt Project for documentation. Upon contacting those black Arkansans, she often found their enthusiasm for the museum's plan matched her own. Notwithstanding their long residence in Louisiana, many still considered Arkansas home and themselves as Arkansans. They were receptive to the idea of installing their quilts in an Arkansas museum where their quilts, in the future, would be put on exhibition.

In the course of assisting the Old State House Museum, Sandra Todaro became more than an intermediary between the Old State House Museum staff and Arkansas black quilters then living in Louisiana. By personally interviewing the quilters at length, gathering abundant information about them, supplying copious field notes to the museum, securing corollary family items, documents, and photographs, Sandra's role expanded to one of an active participant and advisor to the Old State House Museum's project. Due to Sandra's emphasis on chronicling the historical aspects of those black families' quilt works, she obtained more specific data on black Arkansan *quilt-making families,* often reaching back two and three generations, than had been recorded in any previous study of African American quilt-making. For quite a long time numerous reports of white American families' quilt connections have been recorded, but for understandable reasons, seldom have generational black families' quilts been documented. Several years ago the discovery of a multigenerational black quilting family, the Perkins of Trevilians, Virginia, was a time of rejoicing for quilt history researchers because it was such a rare find.[13] Rare, too, is the Old State House Museum's sizeable collection of quilts made by multiple generations of black Arkansan families.

Arkansas's Black Quiltmakers and Their Quilts

Families of Quilters

The Old State House Museum's African American quilt collection is unique for the number and variety of its family quilts. Quilts made by mothers and daughters, sisters, twins, cousins, and three generations, grandmothers, mothers, daughters, are a part of this remarkable assemblage of quilts constructed by black Arkansans. Their family quilts, dated circa 1890 to the present, are representative of almost the entire twentieth century of black quiltmaking in agrarian regions of southern Arkansas. These family quilts have been closely examined for what they reveal about the transmittal of quiltmaking styles and techniques within the family structures. Whether individual creativity consistently took precedence over inherited family customs of quiltmaking was a question requiring extensive investigation. Other relevant factors, such as the age of the quiltmaker when a bedcover was made, and a comparative analysis of her other quilts made at different times, needed probing. Conducting a parallel comparative study of a quilter's kinfolk's quiltworks was also an important component of the research of family quilts.

These groupings of African American quilts reflect a strong tradition practiced in rural areas of Arkansas where the quilters lived. Quilts were deemed a household necessity. Although Arkansas lies within the temperate zone, warm bedding was required for the unheated, drafty, and ofttimes chilly sleeping areas of their homes farm families had to endure. Homemade bedcovers and feather tick mattresses and pillows provided insulation against the cold. Materials for making the quilts were most often scraps of fabric pieced together to form the top. Salvagable pieces of fabrics cut from worn-out clothing, such as men's pants or jeans, were made into heavy, warm "britches" quilts. The interlining or filler was a recycled worn blanket or an old no-longer-usable quilt that could be recovered or "field scraps" of cotton. Brown

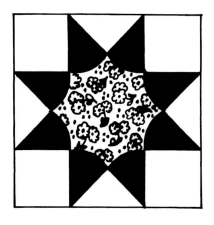

Arkansas Star

or white domestic, feed sacks, and occasionally pieced strips of cloth provided the lining. Some quilts were tied; others were quilted. While several quilt designs appear to have been especially favored by the black Arkansans, such as variations of the Log Cabin, Trip Around the World, and the string quilt, the family quilts in this collection exhibit a wide range of different patterns. It is, however, the interpretations of the quilt designs by black Arkansas quilters that is so captivating.

Mothers fashioned quilts and taught their children including at times their sons to also make quilts. When the children became adults and continued the process of parent-quiltmakers teaching their off-spring the craft, it became a generation-to-generation procedure. Although the tradition of generational quiltmaking was firmly established in rural Arkansas, it has always been difficult to locate early examples of black-made family quilts. Rarely can one trace the lineage of a quilt-producing family such as the Allens who lived near Camden in Quachita County.

The Allen/Williams Family, Camden, Arkansas

David Allen and Mary Ann, former slaves, married in the 1870s and lived in Quachita County, near Camden. They had six known children: Leon (b. 1875), David (b. 1877), Varrie (b. 1880, a girl), Cordelia (b. 1881, nicknamed "Deelie"), James (b. 1885), and Mary (b. 1889). Born also to the couple were other children who died in infancy or childhood and whose names are unknown. Mary Ann, the mother, lived until the mid-1930s; the place and date of death of David, the father, are not known. Family members who died were buried near Camden in a private cemetery reputed to have been the Shiloh Baptist Church burial grounds.

David and Mary Ann's youngest daughter, Mary, had eleven children. Three daughters, twins Tillie Rae and Willie Mae (b. 1914) and Hattie (b. 1918), of Mary Allen Smith Williams became third-generation Allen/Williams family quiltmakers.

Of the three daughters born to Mary Ann and David Allen, two, Cordelia and Mary, were quiltmakers. Cordelia and Mary were archetypes of individual creativity taking precedence over any conformity one would expect their heritage to impose. Quiltworks of the sisters are different in concept and execution.

Cordelia, nee Deelie, Allen Green's quilts display an effective strength of design and a sense of confidence that contains not a hint of timidity in her creative processes. Deelie's quilt, the Texas Star (Plate 1), was made in the late 1920s or early 1930s. She traded butter and eggs for the fabric for the quilt, getting a little at a time until the quilt was completed. The attractive quilt's unusual color scheme of lavender, blue, green, white, and pink is enhanced by the corner "fill-ins." Even more so did Cordelia prove her mastery of the design when she very subtly changed one corner of the top so it was unlike the other three corners. Texas Star was Cordelia Green's best quilt used only on Sundays or on special occasions.

When she was well into her sixties, Cordelia Green pieced her last quilt, the Log Cabin (Plate 2). She had not lost her forthright sense of style. Her quilt, a melange of predominantly crimson, orange, and brown is a dramatic presentation of the Log Cabin design in the courthouse-steps configuration. Cordelia Green died in the mid 1950s and was buried in the same private cemetery as her parents and relatives.

Figure 1. Mary Allen Williams's home, Camden, Arkansas, circa 1920. Acc. no. 95.01.20.

Mary Allen Smith Williams lived the greater part of her life around Fouke, Arkansas. She was married twice, first to a man named Smith, who was considerably older than Mary. His given name is unknown. She was married in 1903 or 1904 when she was about fifteen years old. Her second husband was Sam Williams. The family lived in a four-room dogtrot-style log cabin. Mary was the mother of a very large family and at least eleven of the children lived to adulthood. She had two sets of twins, both sets were girls. She lost three children in the influenza epidemic of 1918. In the 1960s, Mary moved to Los Angeles, California, to live with a daughter, but returned to the Fouke area where she remained until her death in 1971. Her husband Sam's date of death is unconfirmed, but the family believes it was in the 1940s, a number of years prior to Mary's move to California. The Williams family's religious denomination was and still is Baptist.

Although Mary never learned to read or write, she taught all of her daughters to sew and to quilt. Frames for quilting consisted of boards laid over the backs of hide-bottomed chairs. Fabrics for quiltmaking came from leftover sewing scraps, worn-out clothing, and feed, flour, and sugar sacks, as purchasing fabric strictly for a quilt was not done. Very often they would unravel the string in the feed and flour sacks to use for quilting. They wasted absolutely nothing. As the Williams family's finances improved in later years backing fabric was purchased. Batting was scrap cotton gathered after the harvest or what could be picked up on the roadside that blew out of the wagons on their way to the cotton gins. Old quilts were used as filling for new ones and occasionally burlap sacking served as filler. Quilt patterns were obtained from family, friends, magazines, and newspapers, or quilters designed their own patterns. The quilters often called well-known quilt designs by different names peculiar to their local regions.

In most instances, Mary Allen Smith Williams employed a more subdued palette on her quilts than did her sister, Cordelia Green. Yet Mary's quilts were never dull. Instead they were quite lively pieces because of the mixture of colors resulting from her frequent use of innumerable prints and small patches. One of the most arresting of Mary's quilts is the Pine Cone (Plate 3). There are two sections to this Pine Cone that originally comprised the center of the quilt. The sections were sewn together and surrounded by side strips. When the side strips became tattered and were removed, the two Pine Cone sections were separated, and unfortunately, never sewn back together. The Pine Cone, made in the late 1940s or early 1950s, was used by the family as a decorative bedspread not as a utilitarian quilt.

From early to late twentieth century, the Pine Cone quilt was popular among southern African American quilters. Notable examples have been found in Georgia, Alabama, Tennessee, Louisiana, Kentucky, Florida, and Arkansas. Held in high esteem as a masterpiece work, the Pine Cone's position in the black quilt community was analagous to the regard accorded to the intricate appliquéd quilts fashioned by white quiltmakers during the same era. Yet the Pine Cone was not an exclusively black-made quilt. Specimens of this same pattern made by white quiltmakers have surfaced. White quilters' versions, known as the Target or Bull's Eye, usually have southern origins and have been found in Texas, Oklahoma, and North Carolina. Quilt history expert Kathlyn Sullivan believes that black people continued to make Pine Cone quilts long after the majority of white quiltmakers ceased fabricating these novelty works.[1] The Pine Cone is also called the Pine Burr by blacks, especially in Alabama. A woman, China Grove Myles, who was associated with the black cooperative the Freedom Quilting Bee, Gees Bend, Alabama, attained national recognition and legendary status for making the Pine Burr quilts.[2] Widespread newspaper coverage resulted in people all over the country seeking to buy one of her Pine Burr quilts.

The patches of Pine Cone quilts are small squares folded into triangles sewn down on one side only, a similar construction to mainstream American quilters' patches known as "prairie points." The folded triangles placed in ever widening concentric circles are sewn to a base. Thus there are hundreds, even thousands of tiny triangles giving a three dimensional effect to the whole. Because of the total weight of so much fabric sewn onto the top, the finished quilt is extremely heavy. Whatever the color scheme adopted for the top, whether all print, all plain, or a mixture of print and plain, it is almost impossible to make a nonspectacular Pine Cone quilt.[3]

Mary Williams and her daughter, Tillie Rae, pieced and quilted the Diamonds quilt (Plate 4) in the 1950s. Their Diamonds quilt contained numerous leftover fabrics from other sewing projects. Mary and Tillie Rae utilized the same basic diamond patch for constructing all of the blocks. Yet by including a myriad of different prints punctuated by a vivid solid red, and improvisational piecing, each block looks different, not like a replica of the others. The Diamonds quilt then became more like an album quilt. Mary gave the Diamonds quilt to another daughter, Hattie, as a present.

The Tacked Strip Quilt with Center Medallion (Plate 5) was pieced by Mary Williams, circa 1950, but some of the fabrics are from the late 1930s and 1940s. The filling is burlap. Outlined by a wide dark frame the center medallion is surrounded by an interior border of various-sized strips whose colors have softened and mellowed. Inside the dark center frame are both squares of identifiable quilt patterns and randomly cut strips, all in the quiet colorations characteristic of several of Mary's quilts.

Made circa 1940 by Mary Williams, the Log Cabin variation quilt (Plate 6) is one of the oldest quilts of Mary's in the collection. The surviving family did not have a name for the quilt. In some southern black quilt communities the design is called the Pig Pen. By placing soft light-colored print blocks over most of her quilt juxtaposed with five electrifying red and black, red and orange, red, black, and white blocks centered horizontally across the middle of her cover, Mary's Log Cabin quilt becomes a highly graphic composition with a definite focal point.

The muted 16 Patch Quilt (Plate 7) is a recovered quilt by Mary Williams's daughter Hattie. It covers an old worn hexagon strip quilt made earlier by Mary. Three distinct quilt patterns are evident on the 16 Patch top: a wide center strip featuring the four-patch design and serving as borders, a windmill pattern on one side, and a sixteen-patch design on the other. On the top are 1940s lower-decibel-colored fabrics of pale hues of blue, tan, pink, and much white. The backing is of 1960s fabrics. Apparently the recovering of the old quilt occurred in the 1960s.

One of Mary's last quilts was the Triangle Strip (Plate 8) made in the late 1960s or early 1970s. What a plethora of colors and fabrics it contains, offset by sashing in the familiar avocado green, orange, and yellow oversized floral designs that bespeak the tumultuous 1960s and 1970s. Many who experienced those times will remember that ubiquitous color scheme. Avocado green, orange, and yellow, combined or separate, were everywhere; in home furnishings, rugs, floors, walls, large and small kitchen appliances, both ceramic and plastic dinnerware, bolts of fabrics, and ready-made clothing. Mary's Triangle Strip quilt exudes an air of excitement and a sort of confrontational passion. If tying together the turbulent 1960s and its influence on the quilt works of a sixty-year-old black woman in rural Arkansas seems a bit far fetched, one can counter with the argument that there were few Americans who were not affected in some manner by the hectic sixties. The Triangle Strip was possibly Mary's last hurrah, as she died of a heart attack in 1971.

Another favorite quilt design among southern black quilters is the starkly simple, yet dramatic quilt the Mary Williams family called a Log Cabin (Plate 9). In some regions of the South, the pattern of outward-moving squares or rectangles, each encompassing the other, was called a Pig Pen. Mary's Log Cabin quilt was made in the 1950s, though some of the fabrics in it began to be seen in the 1940s. The Log Cabin's physical condition indicates it has seen heavy use. How fortunate it is that a wonderful utilitarian quilt used until it became worn was preserved and was not recycled. It could have suffered the fate of many such quilts by being recovered or cut into pieces to provide padding for other household uses or sewing projects.

One of the most extraordinary pieces in the entire Old State House Museum quilt collection is Mary Williams's doll quilt (Plate 10). In the late 1930s or 1940s, Mary fashioned the little quilt in the Log Cabin design for one of her grandchildren. Assorted scraps of pink check, pink floral, brown plaid, green stripe, blue floral, and blue plaid were sewn into the tiny cover. Judging by its condition the doll quilt had obviously been played with a lot. Rarely have handsewn doll quilts attributed to a black quilter been located. Thus far, the only other documented black-made doll quilts were found in North Carolina reported by Kathlyn Sullivan while working on the North Carolina Quilt Project and by Maude Wahlman conducting independent research on southern African American quilts.[4]

The Strip Diamonds or Slashed Album quilt top (Plate 11) was one of Mary's later efforts, made circa 1960. She still liked working with the diamond quilt patch, so familiar in her earlier quilts. And her preference for working with a multitude of scraps of different designs had not abated. She still maintained the spontaneity that made her a master of organizing countless dissimilar fabric scraps into a pleasing whole. By this time, however, Mary's eyesight was failing. She had a couple of elderly lady friends with whom she would piece and quilt. According to family lore Mary primarily just pieced tops at this stage of her life.

As the years passed, Mary Allen Williams's daughters, Tillie Rae, Willie Mae, and Hattie, often assisted their mother in her quiltmaking

Figure 2. Hattie Williams Jones,
Fouke, Arkansas, circa 1920. Acc. no.
95.01.12.

projects. On their own, and following the family tradition of their mother and Aunt Cordelia, the sisters became quiltmakers.

Hattie Williams Jones, Fouke, Arkansas, was the youngest daughter of Mary Allen Williams. Hattie became a fine seamstress and made clothes for her children and herself. She had the reputation of being the best seamstress in the family. Hattie was a prolific quiltmaker. She made more quilts than her family could use and gave them as Christmas and wedding gifts to her children. Upon marriage, each child received a quilt of Hattie's making. Hattie taught all of her children to sew, just as she had been taught by her mother, Mary. At present, it is believed that none of the women in the family quilts.

The twenty-block quilt made by Hattie in the late 1950s or early 1960s was called the Snowflake (Plate 12) by the family. Hattie traded patterns with her women friends and often cut patterns from the newspapers as well. A similar quilt pattern had been published in 1935 in the *Kansas City Star* newspaper as the Arkansas Snowflake.[5]

Other patterns that perhaps are a closer approximation of Hattie's quilt were commonly called Snowball or Four Points. Like her mother, Hattie did not always feel constrained to reproduce exactly a quilt pattern as printed in a commercial source. While maintaining the general concept of the published Snowflake, Hattie's impromptu changes can be detected in both the quilt blocks and in the construction of the sashing. Each block does contain the four small snowflake motifs, but Hattie's did not make the motifs exact replications of the others as was shown in the newspaper version. By varying the fabrics and colors in the little snowflake motifs and in the block backgrounds, as well as coupling the randomly pieced sashing of at least ten different fabrics, Hattie's Snowflake quilt is an example of two strong influences brought to bear upon her quilt. From her family legacy came the informal, improvisational piecing techniques, and from the published newspaper source came the formal, conventionalized concepts.

Figure 3. The Arkansas Snowflake quilt pattern, published by the *Kansas City Star* (Missouri) on February 13, 1935. The newspaper did have a weekly Arkansas/Oklahoma edition.

The Jumping Jack quilt top (Plate 13) was made by Hattie and two of her sisters in the early 1950s. The Jumping Jack is the prototype of a "fool the eye" quilt. At first glance it appears to be a multiple-patterned or an album quilt because diverse patterns such as Fly Foot, Swastika, Rolling Star, and Ring Around the Star emerge on the quilt top. *Yet, Hattie and her sisters used the exact same design on each block!* The sizes of their patches of diamonds, triangles, and squares within the blocks are uniform. The essential structure of the blocks did not vary. It was the arrangement of the colors on a block that caused the different quilt designs to appear. Experienced quilters have long known this chameleon-like occurrence would happen, and Hattie and her sisters were experienced quiltmakers. They understood that simply changing the color placement of one design would produce several disparate designs. Evidently the sisters experimented making a number of different designs from their Jumping Jack pattern. It would seem the sisters probably pieced more experimental blocks than they needed for this quilt top. For at the head of the quilt, they placed four experimental blocks they were compelled to cut in half, in order to make the quilt top the size that was needed. No one in the family knows why this top was never quilted.

When Hattie Williams Jones and her mother, Mary, made the Flower Garden quilt (Plate 14), they were utilizing one of the oldest designs in the American quiltmaker's lexicon. Early in the nineteenth century this hexagonal design called Mosaic or Honeycomb was in great favor with American quiltmakers. It was, however, in the twentieth century that the design, renamed Grandmother's Flower Garden, reached the zenith of its popularity. By the 1930s, Grandmother's Flower Garden was featured prominently in newspapers, magazines, and pattern pamphlets and as precut quilt kits. It was during this period that Mary pieced the rosettes that are in the main body of the quilt. Years later, circa 1970, Hattie completed the quilt by adding the hexagons seen at the bottom of the quilt. She also added the familiar "paths" associated with Flower Garden quilts. Hattie's and Mary's quilt does not look like the usual, prim Flower Garden quilts made by mainstream American quilters. The mother-daughter duo's exuberant quilt has oversized hexagons, probably for the same practical reasons expressed by a black Mississippi-born quiltmaker Malverna Richardson when she made a Flower Garden quilt:

> My mama didn't raise no fools. I used to make those litle bitty hexagons, but no more! I make them big now because it's easier and I can get done with the quilt in half the time![6]

Nor did Hattie and Mary follow the fashion of framing the hexagon rosettes with the ubiquitous "green paths" seen on so many 1930s pastel Flower Garden quilts. Their substitution of a bright turquoise blue path intensifies the colors of the hexagon rosettes, making them much more vivid. The Flower Garden is a very thick quilt of home-carded cotton batting, with quilting stitches measuring about three per inch. Some of the fabrics are polyester double knits.

Hattie Williams Jones's twin-sized Star of Bethlehem (Plate 15) was pieced as recently as 1986. By placing wide dark-green bands atop and underneath the large central star, Hattie effectively anchored the star to the quilt top, rather than to have the appearance of a freely floating star, as so often is the case. Impressive, too, is the carefully cut red-and-white-striped material surrounding the outer circle of the star's center. It adds a subtle twinkle to the design. The quilt has a thin batting and is quilted in colored thread, four to six stitches per inch. A pink bedsheet serves as the quilt's lining.

Certain basic quilt patterns such as the Nine Patch, Brick, Lazy Gal, and randomly pieced strip quilts were endemic to southern rural black households. Some persons would term the informally pieced scrap quilts, the Brick and the Lazy Gal, as strip quilts. For the truly initiated, however, there were discernible and identifiable differences between the patterns. The Brick quilt consisted of rectangular patches set in rows, each row staggered from the next, like brick masonry. How rigidly a quilt conformed to the general Brick design concept depended upon the quiltmaker's purposes, skills, and available fabric cache. For the most part, these scrap quilts were casually constructed. If a patch were square instead of having a rectangular shape, it would, nevertheless, be sewn into a row of the Brick quilt because the size and shape of the brick patch was determined by the scraps available at the time of sewing. The overall visual impact of the quilt mattered most and not minor details such as whether a brick patch in a row had a square or rectangular shape. Once placed on a bed, the completed scrap quilt with its myriad of colors and prints presented a pretty picture admired by the quiltmaker and her family alike.

Hattie Jones's Brick quilt (Plate 16) was made of multiple pieces of polyester double knits, with a blue sheet backing lapped over to the front to make a four-and-one-half-inch border. The Brick quilt was pieced in 1975. In discussing this quilt, the family reported that Hattie was a believer in evil spirits. As to whether that belief had any significance to the making of the quilt in variable shapes is not known.

The Jacob's Ladder and 16 Patch quilt (Plate 17) because of its coloration is an optical illusion quilt. Its light colors have a shadowy effect over the dark prints and brilliant orange. It appears the pale Jacob's Ladder design overlays the 16 Patch segment of the pattern. This is an example of a complex manipulation of piecing and colors that differs markedly from most mainstream white Americans' version of a shadow quilt. Mainstream quilters use another actual layer of thin, almost transparent, white organdy or lawn cloth atop a block to give the quilt a hazy look, and such a quilt is known as a shadow quilt. Hattie's quilt had no overlay of a separate fabric. Her quilt was pieced in a manner that is more akin to today's fashionable concept of using gradations of color from bright to pale. Hattie's small quilt has a thin batting and a dark blue-gray bedsheet lining and was quilted four to six stitches per inch. She pieced this unusual quilt in 1986.

For her Nine Patch quilt top (Plate 18), Hattie Jones grouped four nine-patch squares in each of thirty 14-inch blocks. She pieced the multicolored nine patches and the two-inch royal blue sashing of polyester double knits. Hattie did not quilt the Nine Patch because she intended it to be used as a bedspread.

Tillie Rae Williams Hall and Willie Mae Williams Smith, twin sisters of Hattie Jones, made this tacked giant Log Cabin quilt (Plate 19) in the courthouse steps configuration, circa 1940. It was in Willie Mae's possession when she died. The family stated that Willie Mae was living near Camden, Arkansas, at the time of her death. She did not have any children. Her husband is believed to have worked for a paper mill in Camden.

When Tillie Rae Hall pieced her Lazy Gal quilt (Plate 20), she was using one of the most well-known quilt constructions in the southern rural black quiltmakers' repertoire. Her Lazy Gal is a recovered quilt as there is another quilt inside, which probably explains why she tacked the quilt with green embroidery floss rather than to quilt it. The old quilt inside used for batting made her Lazy Gal thick, weighty, and sturdy. Tillie Rae pieced the top of colorful polyester double knits and cotton blends and made a multipieced lining of muslin and flannel. Her Nine Patch was made circa 1970.

The Wilson Family, Calion, Arkansas

Frances Smith Wilson and Melvin Wilson, married circa 1900. Frances Smith was born in the late 1800s and died in 1948. Both Frances Smith Wilson and her husband were born in Arkansas, exact locations unknown. Frances married Melvin Wilson at age thirteen, and eleven children were born to the couple. The Wilson family lived near Calion, Arkansas. Frances and Melvin Wilson were buried in a black Baptist cemetery in Union County, but there are no grave markers.

All of Frances Wilson's children were taught to sew and four of her daughters, Authorine (b. 1912), Eldora (b. 1915), Minnie Ola (b. 1917), and Welthia (b. 1918), became excellent quiltmakers. Frances was a quiltmaker, and she made numerous quilts during her lifetime. Not much remains of her handiwork because over the years her quilts were worn out. Most of her quilts were tied, as Frances did not like the quilting process.

A surviving quilt of Frances Wilson is her Star of Lemoyne quilt (Plate 21) pieced during the middle 1930s. Frances called the pattern Lemon Star, a common corruption for the name LeMoyne of Jean Baptiste LeMoyne, Sieur de Bienville, the founder of New Orleans in 1718. This quilt contains scraps so tiny that some of the points of the stars, themselves, were pieced. Onto the pieced border a once red but now faded and worn binding was attached. The Star of LeMoyne quilt was tacked with red and orange yarn ties. The back is sacking material pieced to make it larger. Sacking is called "croker sacks" in a number of rural southern communities.

Authorine Wilson married Willie T. Anderson when she was sixteen years of age. She had four children who lived to adulthood. One son was killed while on duty in the armed services. During the last twenty-five years of her life Authorine Anderson lived near Alexandria, Louisiana. Her husband was employed in the timber industry and worked at a sawmill. Authorine died in 1996.

Authorine liked to piece and appliqué, but after she was afflicted with arthritis, she could no longer sew by hand. She began to use a sewing machine to make quilt tops. Others including her sister Welthia and the women in her church group would do the quilting. Authorine's Butterfly quilt (Plate 22) is one of a few appliquéd quilts in the collection. In each of the quilt's fifteen butterfly blocks, various colors and fabrics were used. Because of a variance in the sizes and shapes of the butterflies, there is a suggestion that perhaps Authorine cut the motifs "by eye."

Quilt scholar Sandra Todaro's report of her interview with Eldora Wilson contains a wealth of first-person information. Dr. Todaro wrote:

> I did manage to finally make contact with Eldora, whose married name is Mrs. Tom Thomas, and went to see her when she came to her daughter's home last week. She lives outside Texarkana, Texas. She told me she was going to be 81 this September. Her husband is deceased and has been for quite some time. . . .
>
> To say this lady is a prolific textile artist is an understatement. She quilts, sews, crochets, tats, and heaven only knows what else. I spent quite an enjoyable afternoon with her. There were nearly 20 quilts of her manufacture at her daughter's house alone. She says she has no idea how many quilts she has made over her lifetime, but it's "considerable." Sewing is more than a hobby for her; it's an avocation. She told me she loves to feel the fabrics in her hands and play with the different colors until she gets just the combination she wants. She said she has been known to rip out a piece if she felt it spoiled the look of her top. Mrs. Thomas works with both scraps and purchased lengths of cloth, but does not like to use old clothing in her work, as she states (rightly so) that the used materials won't hold up next to the new ones, and wear out much faster. She did say, she had done this in the past when her children were

small and finances were tighter. Then she would use whatever she could get her hands on to make bed covers. She refers to them as "kivvers." I have heard this expression before among older quilters, both black and white. I do think it is Southern terminology, a "Southernism" as my husband calls them.

She did not mind selling me one of her quilts, though she said she had never sold one before. I explained my interest and what was going to be done with the quilt, and she seemed quilte pleased at the prospect. Each quilt was displayed for me and its merits and flaws discussed. I chose this one for its graphic appeal and the unusual name she ascribed to the pattern. She called it "Boxed Star." I have never encountered this name before . . . and it may well be a true regional name for this pattern.[7]

The Boxed Star quilt (Plate 23), made in the mid-1960s by Eldora Wilson Thomas, daughter of Frances Wilson, is in a mint, unwashed condition. It was never used because of the sheer volume of work output by the maker. Its blocks of plain dark-blue stars set in a "box" of print materials make a graphic composition, completed by the same print placed on two narrow, inner borders at the top and bottom of the quilt. Eldora's traditional patterned quilt has a very contemporary look.

Frances Wilson's third quiltmaking daughter, Minnie Ola Wilson Leary, lived near El Dorado most of her life. She and her husband, LB Leary (no period between the L and the B), farmed for a living. Minnie Leary died in the late 1960s of a heart attack. She had no surviving children, but there are grandchildren in that family.

Minnie Ola Leary's forceful, bright red-dominated Pinwheel quilt (Plate 24) is actually a summer spread, as it has no batting. The setting block to block of the pinwheels with no intervening sashing allows a secondary pattern to form on the quilt top. Moreover, Minnie Ola at times pieced the individual spokes of the pinwheels in two different fabrics, allowing a tertiary design to appear, as if the quilt contained pinwheels of different sizes. Additionally, each pinwheel square is pieced in a different color arrangement, dominated by plain red, so the entire quilt takes on the look of a maze or a puzzle. Minnie Ola's Pinwheel quilt is a striking example of how, with a few changes, a simple pieced pattern can manifest itself as an extraordinarily complex work. It anticipated or presaged the highly regarded art or studio quilts of today. Minnie Ola's Pinwheel quilt is one of the most inventive and original specimens of pieced patchwork in the collection.

Figure 4. Eldora Wilson Thomas, circa 1920. Acc. no. 95.01.2.

Born in April 1918 near the community of Calion, Arkansas, Welthia Wilson Wardlaw was the youngest of Frances Wilson's quilt-making daughters. Welthia Wilson married Cedric Wardlaw in 1938, and seven children were born to that union, five of whom are still living. After Cedric Wardlaw died in 1990, Welthia Wardlaw moved to Shreveport, Louisiana, to live with her daughter. Making quilts has always been an integral part of Welthia's life, and although the pressing needs of earlier years no longer exist, she continues to make the covers. She does so to pass the time and to create beauty out of scraps and leftovers. Welthia does not believe her grandchildren value her quilts. They see quilts as a link to an impoverished past and prefer the store-bought blankets. She, on the other hand, recognizes the quilts for what they are, a connection to her heritage. In a hard early life often devoid of extra money, quilts provided a bit of beauty as well as a way to warm her family. Today she owns quilt books that show a variety of different patterns, but she prefers to use patterns she learned from her mother or ones she devises herself. Welthia's favorite patterns are the Fancy Plate (a form of the Dresden Plate), the Log Cabin, and the Strippy quilt.

In 1989, Welthia's daughter bought a quilt block at a garage sale. With its deep rich coloration, the block closely resembles a miniaturized version of the Amish Center Diamond pattern. Welthia placed the block in the center of her quilt, surrounded it with fairly wide strips in colors of the deep hues that harmonized with the purchased block. In the corners of her quilt, she placed four nine-patch squares. Each nine-patch square contained dark-colored patches alternating with striped patches, stripes cut on the diagonal. It is a highly effective, original quilt that has a coloration reminiscent of the Amish, but not a design associated with the Plain People. Welthia Wardlaw's Central Medallion quilt (Plate 25) is a virtuoso work.

Commonalities shared by the Wilson family quilters are a true creative response to their quiltmaking, with a keen, almost uncanny sense of color and an ability to adeptly organize the spaces. Their quilts attest to the substantial influence of the mother, Frances Wilson.

The Collins/Wilson Family, Magnolia, Arkansas

In reconstructing the Collins/Wilson family saga, we encountered a very common occurrence in the family quiltmaking tradition, the skipping of one generation of quilt-interested relatives in a family line. In this family, the grandmother was an ardent quilter; her daughter did not like quiltmaking; and yet third-generation granddaughters took to the craft with great zeal.

Hattie Collins was born a slave on a plantation near Arkadelphia, Arkansas. While living on the plantation as a young child, Hattie was taught to sew and quilt. After the Civil War, she continued to live in Arkadelphia until she was grown. Subsequently, Hattie married a carpenter who was also a former slave. She and her husband quite often moved about in search of work. They had several children (actual number unknown), most of whom died in infancy. Four of their children lived to adulthood, one of whom was Lucy, who married Herman Wilson. Years later, Hattie Collins moved to the Magnolia, Arkansas, home of Lucy and Herman Wilson and stayed with her daughter's family. During the time Hattie lived with Lucy and Herman, she pieced countless quilts and she also taught her granddaughter Herma, an apt pupil, to make quilts. Despite having a quilting mother and daughter, Lucy Wilson never wanted to be a quiltmaker. The family reported that Lucy made only one quilt in her life. Hattie Collins died in the 1930s.

Slave-made quilts are extremely difficult to locate today, especially those quilts that remained in the hands of the quiltmakers. More slave-made quilts that remained with the slave owners have been preserved. (A quilt cannot accurately be termed a slave-made quilt unless it was constructed prior to the time the slave quiltmaker was emancipated.) Even searching for quilts made by former slaves during the postbellum period, 1865–1890, can prove to be a daunting task. Quilts were made to be used, and given the fragile nature of textiles and the poverty-stricken living conditions of most of the former slaves during the post-bellum era, the likelihood of finding a suriving quilt from this time is not good. Countless quilts made by former slaves for household use were either worn out from use or were recycled, either as recovered quilts or as other smaller household items requiring padded surfaces.

Of the numerous quilts Hattie Collins, a former slave, made in her lifetime, only one is extant. Old, fragile, and much used, her Log Cabin quilt (Plate 26) is appealing, nevertheless, with its soft colors faded by many washings. Hattie pieced this Log Cabin circa 1900.

Born to Lucy and Herman Wilson, Herma Wilson Williams grew up around Magnolia in Columbia County, Arkansas, where her parents were sharecroppers or tenant farmers. She was named for her father, Herman. By learning to quilt as a child Herma had completed her first quilt by age eight. She recalled that during her childhood her family raised brown cotton to use as batting for quilts. Even as an adult, she always raised a special patch of cotton exclusively for quilting use. After ginning, she carded the cotton for batting. Her quilting frame consisted of four boards nailed together, then placed on chair backs.

Prior to Herma Wilson's marriage in the late 1930s to Ray Williams, a farmer, she pieced a marriage or dowry quilt. It was the "H" quilt (Plate 27), circa 1930, of twenty 11-inch square blocks. The "H" denoted the first letter in her given name, Herma. When asked why she made the quilt, Herma replied, "Because I wanted to." She made the quilt from a pattern copied from a magazine or a newspaper. Herma considered the "H" quilt the best of her work.

The American Tree quilt (Plate 28), circa 1940, included twenty squares of red, blue, orange, gold, and green tree motifs separated by two-inch red sashing, intersected by small blue squares, and quilted eight or nine stitches to an inch. Whereas Herma Williams may have thought of her "H" quilt as her best work she said the American Tree was her favorite. She was not the sole person who admired this quilt. An antiques dealer in Louisiana eagerly sought the American Tree quilt. Only when Sandra Todaro explained to Mrs. Williams that the American Tree would be in a museum in her home state of Arkansas, on view for many people to see, did the quilt eventually join the Old State House Museum quilt collection.

Herma set her blue and white Snowball quilt (Plate 29) block to block with no intervening sashing. She termed the Snowball "a utility quilt" made because "we needed covers." The quilt was made from Bull Durham tobacco sacks. Ray, Herma's husband, rolled his own cigarettes. For two years, Herma saved the little sacks in which loose tobacco came so she would have enough fabric for a quilt top. She then bleached and hand dyed the sacks. She gave the quilt a thick batting and quilted it four to five stitches per inch.

In an unusual set of circumstances, Herma acquired the Snowball quilt pattern. She said: "The Snowball pattern came from some newspapers wrapped around some fish. I dried it in the sun, then cut me the pattern from it."[8]

In 1957, Herma and Ray Williams moved to Shreveport, where he got a job as a laborer with a northern Louisiana pipeline company. Herma saved some quilt patterns as fragment blocks she'd brought from Arkansas. She said she "intended to use them someday." Examples of the blocks Herma saved are the Dutch Doll, in other regions frequently called the Sunbonnet Girl; a Kite quilt fragment (Plate 30); and a String quilt fragment, with paper base shown (Plate 31). In Arkansas, she'd pieced traditional patterns such as Strippy quilts, but had none left. Asked which quilts she liked best to make, she replied, "Nine Patch quilts because they go so fast." In 1988, Herma Williams moved to Los Angeles, California, to live with her daughter.

Hattie Collins also taught another grandchild, Essie, to sew and quilt. Essie was Herma's cousin; their mothers were sisters. Essie was born in 1891 on a farm in the Magnolia, Arkansas, area. She married George Jackson, and sometime after World War II, they moved from Arkansas. Essie Jackson died in 1987 at the age of ninety-six. She had no children, and so two quilts of Essie's making were given to her cousin, Herma Williams.

The Dutch Tile quilt top (Plate 32), an unquilted top inherited by Herma, was pieced by Essie Jackson, Columbia County, Arkansas, circa 1940. The Dutch Tile is an example of improvisational piecing and setting and until recently would have been simply called a "country quilt." Some rural quilters are noted for being able to cut directly into the cloth, without the use of a template or measuring to develop a pattern. It is called "cutting by eye." Improvisational quilters do not feel compelled to conform to imposed standard quilting conventions. Uniformity of blocks and of set are not a high-priority goal. The quilters' paramount purpose is to make warm bedcovers for their family and to use whatever materials they have on hand. If there's insufficient material of one color to complete a border the quilter improvises by piecing in another fabric or perhaps several different fabrics in order to finish the task. If a pieced block turned out to be smaller than the other pieced blocks that were to be placed on the quilt, why not add a strip to the smaller block to make it larger? Improvisation is governed by pragmatism as much as by the lyrical and fanciful reasons offered by some scholars. Essie's Dutch Tile has a number of various-sized squares, some of which have been enhanced by additional strips. Rather than to state that a quilter like Essie made her quilt in such a manner because she was compelled by an unconscious cultural memory to do so, it would perhaps be more accurate to say that Essie very consciously knew exactly what was needed. Whatever problems her quilt presented, she improvised to solve them.

When Essie made her Double Wedding Ring quilt (Plate 33), circa 1950, she was fabricating her version of one of the most popular American quilt designs of the twentieth century. Thousands of Double Wedding Ring quilts in all kinds of versions have been made in America. Essie's quilt follows the traditional concept, and yet her individual creativity can be seen as she subtly made her "rings" aggressive and recessive to the eye by their coloration. By consistently using the lighter pale colors on the inner rings of the Double Wedding Ring design, the inner rings appear to recede. The outer rings of the design contain the bolder, stronger colors, and so those rings appear to advance. Essie's quilt was pieced of red, light blue, dark blue, yellow, pink, lavender, and orange cotton scraps. An electric blue lining, a medium batting, and quilting stitches in blue thread, five stitches to the inch, completed Essie Jackson's Double Wedding Ring quilt.

The Parker/Hall Family, Emerson, Arkansas

Sally Anna Ingram was born circa 1900 in southern Arkansas, exact location unknown. At age sixteen, Sally Anna married Robert Parker, a sharecropper. She lost several babies during pregnancy, and only one child, Catherine, reached maturity. Sally Anna was an inveterate seamstress; her sewing efforts included quiltmaking. During the time Catherine was a teenager, Sally Anna and Robert Parker decided to give up farming and search for other work. They moved from the Emerson, Arkansas, area to Haynesville, Louisiana, where they became domestic workers for a private family. Sally Anna served as housekeeper, and Robert was the gardener-handyman. As she continued to sew, Sally Anna accumulated lots of fabric scraps, some given to her by her employers. She made quilts for her family as well as for the white family for whom she worked. Sally Anna Parker died of a heart attack in the late 1950s.

When living in Emerson, Sally Anna pieced the vivacious, multi-colored scrap quilt Little Boy's Britches (Plate 34), circa 1930. By setting the quilt block to block with no sashing, the melange of colors presents a virtual labyrinth when searching for the basic square. Inside Sally Anna's Little Boy's Britches is another old quilt used as batting.

Catherine Parker was born in 1931 near Emerson, Arkansas. She was reared by her grandmother, who taught her to quilt. At age sixteen, she married and soon after moved across the border into Louisiana. Catherine Parker Hall has two sons and several grandchildren and is now a widow.

Catherine Hall still quilts. Over the years she has experienced all kinds of quiltmaking. From the early time of her grandmother's quilting instructions to working on joint projects with her quiltmaking mother, Sally Anna, to working independently, now Catherine has developed her own unique style. She does not use standard quilt patterns, per se, but chooses "to play with her fabrics" until it looks right to her. For the quilt's lining, she likes to use bedsheets because they are cheaper than new material purchased by the yard. In former years, Catherine used cotton batting, but now she chooses polyester batting as it is fluffier and does not clump. She always preferred piecing to quilting, and polyester batts do not require as much or as close quilting.

An example of Catherine Parker Hall's "playing with fabrics" and not using standard patterns is her Flag Strip quilt (Plate 35), circa 1990.

Pieced in patriotic colors, the Flag Strip quilt is her original design. In the center of the quilt is an American flag print, and its borders are alternating bands of red, white, and blue. The high loft batting is obviously polyester and is quilted four stitches to the inch. The Flag Strip quilt is Catherine Parker Hall's imaginative response to playing with fabrics.

Perhaps it may appear to be stretching the definition of "family" to include the names of in-laws as family members. Yet in many rural black communities the claims of kinship seem to have very elastic boundaries. The reverence paid by African Americans to the tradition of the extended family is part of their cultural heritage from Africa that was greatly enhanced during the days of slavery in America and continues to varying degrees until today. By rural Arkansas standards, Oscar Evans, who is a cousin by marriage to Catherine Parker Hall, does belong to the Parker-Hall family group.

Oscar Evans was born in 1908 near Emerson, Arkansas. He was one of twelve children born to Beulah and Leon Evans, sharecropping farmers. Oscar's mother was a quiltmaker, and he remembers that she quilted on frames resting on the backs of straight chairs or with the quilt laying directly on the bed. When Oscar grew up, he became a farmer and a carpenter. In the 1920s he married for the first time, wedding Cassie Jones of Claiborne Parish, Louisiana. The couple had seven children, all but two of whom are now deceased. Life was hard for Oscar in the 1920s and 1930s. In order to feed his family he often worked in the fields until dark and then went on to other jobs in the evenings. His wife, Cassie, died in the mid-1940s. Oscar was married for the second time to a widow, Margaret Sudds, in 1952. There were no children from his second marriage. After Margaret died in the mid-1970s, Oscar has lived alone.

The Pine Cone quilt (Plate 36) was pieced by Oscar Evans, circa 1984. He has a blue ribbon indicating a first prize conferred on his quilt in a local contest about 1986. Oscar's Pine Cone was pieced after he had helped his cousin, Catherine Parker Hall, make one for herself. He liked hers so well that the two combined forces to make one for him. It took over six months to complete, as they worked on it intermittently. His and Catherine's Pine Cones are the only two quilts of this design he has ever made or helped to make. Oscar always treasured his Pine Cone quilt, kept it wrapped in a sheet, placed in a closet, and only brought out to show to others.

Southern black quiltmakers are not the only ones who love and admire this wondrous, colorful, three-dimensional Pine Cone quilt. It has also found favor with quilt collectors, quilt dealers, and museum curators. Laura Fisher, an antiques dealer, owns one of these circa 1930 quilts, called the Target, made in Kentucky by a black woman, Bertha McWilliams. In her book, *Quilts of Illusion,* Laura Fisher wrote:

> This Afro-American bedcover is the only quilt in this book whose entire surface is actually three-dimensional . . . Thousands of one-inch "prairie points" or "porcupine quills" (the folded triangles of fabric which are the patches) combine in a scheme of great drama and energy. The central image of a vortex or comet draws the eye in . . . The tactile surface results from sewing the points only at their base, leaving the tips free to overlap the previous rows. The points face inward and are aligned by color to enhance the sense of tumultous vortex.[9]
>
> The eccentric examples . . . are so unusual and out of the ordinary that they defy ready categorization. The Depression-era Target quilt . . . is a highly original composition whose inspiration appears to have come from no readily identifiable source.[10]

The Shed/Bennett Family, Camden, Arkansas

When citing the record of the Shed-Bennett family's quilts to illustrate the durability of a black Arkansan family's quiltmaking heritage, by inference other black family folkways are revealed. The integral role of the extended family in the black family structure and the coping mechanisms developed by black families to overcome impoverished circumstances are factors in the Shed-Bennett family narrative. A wider view of their lives places this family in its cultural, historical, and socioeconomic context.

A direct line of quilters in the Shed-Bennett family can be traced from the grandmother, Asia, to the daughter, Malsie, to the granddaughter, Myrtle. Asia Cummings Shed, and her daughters, Malsie and Pearl, and her granddaughter, Myrtle, were native Arkansans, who lived near Camden. Asia, a needlewoman, also made quilts. Her quilts were utility covers, yet as early as the turn of the century, or slightly before, certain ones of Asia's quilts were treasured. Those special quilts did not receive hard use, and today, one hundred years later, they are in a remarkable state of preservation for quilts made by black people in rural Arkansas.

The Stars quilt (Plate 37), circa 1890–1910, by Asia Cummings Shed was considered a "show piece," used only on special occasions. Its varicolored pieced diamonds make the quilt sparkle. Asia's relatively narrow sashing provides the perfect, unobtrusive frame for the large brilliant star blocks. She was especially adept at choosing appropriate sashing to complement a pieced block's beauty. The Stars is quilted in a utility style called shell or waves, a common type of quilting in the late nineteenth and twentieth centuries.

Pieced by Asia at approximately the same time period was the familiar design, the Lily quilt (Plate 38), circa 1890–1910. Asia, however, transformed the design from the familiar to the unusual by the changes she made. Most often the Lily block is set straight on so the crossed stems of the pieced flower appear on the block as diagonals. Asia set the Lily block on point, and the crossed stems then appeared to form a Roman cross. Her separating sashing was in a zigzag form, a favorite set in the nineteenth century. Other names applied to this set were Bounding Betty and Streak of Lightning.

Malsie Shed married a Mr. Bennett from Texas, and the couple's three children were born in Camden, Arkansas. Malsie's mother, a widow, moved in with the Bennetts and continued to live with them until her death. Malsie, like her mother, was a quiltmaker. She pieced numerous utilitarian quilts for family use. Her quilt frames that sat on the back of straight chairs were held together with large screw clamps. At night the frames were rolled up and stood in the corner of the room. Malsie wasted nothing. For her quilts she used sewing scraps, leftover clothing scraps, sugar and flour sacks, and other fabrics. Perhaps due to the influence of her mother, Malsie also viewed some of her quilts as prized possessions that should be saved from hard wear.

The Yo-yo bedspread (Plate 39), circa 1920–1930, by Malsie Shed Bennett was a novelty type of handwork that became a fad in the early decades of the twentieth century. The Yo-yo's origin dates back to the nineteenth century when they were called rosettes, but not until later did enthusiasm for making them become a craze. Yo-yo pillows, throws, and decorations on clothing and on bedspreads were seen in dry-goods stores, needlework stores, and at county fair competitions. It was an easy design to make and was ideal for using a plethora of fabric scraps. The making of yo-yos was basically a national mainstream fad that soon reached black communities in outlying, remote areas of rural Arkansas.

Figure 5. Malsie Shed Bennett, Camden, Arkansas, circa 1930. Acc. No. 96.01.18.

While most yo-yo spreads are composed of assorted print circles incidentally placed, Malsie's Yo-yo bedspread has an additional planned decorative element. There are two large border rows of lavender cotton in the main body and in the two smaller rectangles at the top of her cover. Her bedspread is in pristine condition and seems never to have been used (Plate 40, detail of Yo-yo).

Malsie contributed to the family income by sewing clothing and doing alterations for customers. In the early 1940s the entire family including the grandmother, Asia, moved to south Texas near Beaumont. Malsie Shed Bennett's husband went to work at an oil refinery, while Malsie continued her sewing and alterations for customers, some of whom were her husband's co-workers. She worked at a cleaners for a while. Malsie accumulated scraps from her work that seem to be suitings fabrics from both men's and women's fashions of the 1930s and 1940s. These dressmaker/tailor scraps were incorporated into her quilts.

The Log Cabin quilt (Plate 41), circa 1930–1950, pieced by Malsie Shed Bennett is set in the courthouse-steps configuration. But with her inventive eye and color placement Malsie's Log Cabin does not look like an ordinary, run-of-the-mill Log Cabin quilt. Hers has mysterious, almost solid-dark sections of color strategically placed on the quilt top. Given the Shed-Bennett quilting women's custom of paying careful attention to detail, it is difficult to assume these pronounced dark sections on the Log Cabin top resulted from mere happenstance. Every other color placement on the top seems almost painstakingly planned. So those four dark portions, symetrically placed at the top, on the right side, on the left side, and in the middle of the quilt's base, will continue to mystify.

Malsie's Log Cabin is pieced in the traditional manner with the blocks sewn to a backing fabric. Each block has a red center which signifies the hearth or fireplace of a log cabin. Certain log strips are pieced of extremely small bits of fabric that have been sewn together to create larger sections, a practice that reaffirms the idea that Malsie wasted nothing. There is no batting in Malsie's Log Cabin quilt. This often occurs when the Log Cabin blocks are already sewn to a base fabric. If a lining is then sewn to the back to cover the stitches on the base fabric, the quilt may become too heavy and unwieldly. Malsie's quite graphic Log Cabin is finely crafted and creative, albeit with its aura of mystery.

A powerful statement about continuity and tradition in the Shed-Bennett family is embodied in the following two quilts made by Malsie Shed Bennett and her daughter, Myrtle Bennett. Both quilts are in the same design, Trip Around the World, and yet they were made over thirty-five years apart. The Trip Around the World is an intricate geometric design requiring hundreds of small pieces of cloth, precisely pieced.

The Trip Around the World quilt (Plate 42), circa 1940, pieced by Malsie Shed Bennett is an unusual composition of the familiar conventional design by that name. The usual Trip Around the World quilt is an all-over configuration of the entire top of small squares radiating outward in different colored rows from a center square. Malsie's conception is a number of blocks, each constituting a small Trip Around the World square. In fact, Malsie's top has one hundred and twenty of the self-contained Trip Around the World blocks. Again her fine color sense came into play, as the colors in each block were harmoniously assembled. She set her quilt block to block, but without the loss of the defining pattern that frequently occurs when so many different block colors are placed next to each other. Malsie very cleverly maintained the integrity of the quilt pattern by surrounding the blocks with a white or light-colored frame. The frames, made of the same small squares set on point of the Trip Around the World blocks served two purposes. They appeared to be both horizontal and vertical sashing, as well as defining each of the one hundred and twenty blocks of this colorful and thoughtfully conceived quilt.

The Trip Around the World quilt, circa 1975, was made by Myrtle Bennett, daughter of Malsie Shed Bennett. Perhaps Myrtle chose this pattern because it was familiar to her from her mother's quilt. Nevertheless, Myrtle's quilt is not identical to the quilt made in the same design nearly three decades earlier. Myrtle's quilt is made of polyester fabrics; her mother's was made of cotton. But the color manipulation and the precise piecing of Myrtle's quilt are reminiscent of Malsie's works. Myrtle did not quilt her Trip Around the World quilt. A group of women at a senior citizens' center quilted her intricate piece.

Myrtle was born and reared in Camden, Arkansas, but lived the last thirty years of her life in Mississippi, near Jackson. She pieced the Trip Around the World top when her husband lay ill and dying. Myrtle nursed him, and as she was required to stay home most of the time, she pieced quilts to help pass the hours. Myrtle died in 1965. Malsie's and Myrtle's Trip Around the World quilts constitute a compelling testimony as to continuity and tradition within the Shed-Bennett family. It is a testimony repeated in the quilt works of other black Arkansas families cited: the Allen-Williams of Camden; the Wilsons of Calion; the Collins-Wilsons of Magnolia; and the Parker-Halls of Emerson.

Individuals

Quilt nomenclature has long been a subject of great curiosity and vigorous discussions. Over the years both traditional quilt and quilting patterns have acquired a multitude of names. It is common knowledge in America some quilt pattern names were invented by the quilt's designer, others came from commercially published sources, while still other names are of unknown origin. Especially interesting and oftentimes colorful are the idiomatic names given to quilts in specific regions. Conferring upon a quilt the name of a familiar object instead of using the generally accepted title of the quilt seemed reasonable to rural quilters. For example, in the early decades of the twentieth century, a certain version of the Grandmother's Fan pattern was called Rooster Tails by some Arkansas black farm women. (Not all versions of Grandmother's Fan were alike, and much of the differences depended on the quilt's set.) To those country women, a rooster was more commonplace than the image of a so-called grandmother's fan. The kind of fans most recognizable to those black women were the noncollapsible ones they saw and used at their local churches during hot summer days. Primarily undertakers but other businesses, too, furnished flat cardboard fans to area churches as a subtle advertising vehicle. Printed on the fans were the names and addresses and perhaps a slogan of the business establishments. Absent from the design of the donated pasteboard fans were the sharply curved segmented sections or "vanes" that are integral to one variant of the pattern Grandmother's Fan's image. If the curved vanes of the fan quilt pattern reminded the quilter of a rooster's tail, which she saw daily, and not of the kind of fan she used to cool herself at church services, her name choice of Rooster Tails for the quilt was an almost foregone conclusion.

The Rooster Tails or Grandmother's Fan quilt (Plate 43) was made by Verily Hopkins, DeQueen, Arkansas, circa 1930. Verily was an ardent Baptist and to her friends she was known as "Sister Hopkins." Devout female members of a number of black Protestant denominations were frequently honored by being called "Sister." Usually the title was applied so frequently that within and outside of the church community the person was known throughout the neighborhood as Sister, instead of Miss or Mrs. When Verily Hopkins died in the early 1980s, all of her children had preceded her in death, and so her few remaining quilts were given to one of her dear friends.

Arkansas Meadow Rose

The Rooster Tails quilt has a multiple-pieced binding and a solid-white backing and was hand quilted four to six stitches per inch on a thin batt. Apparently it was a much-used quilt, as it is very worn and has some staining. Its sixteen-pieced blocks are of calico and cream "fans" or vanes with black points, and because of their separated curving shapes, the quilt has a lively look. Alternating squares that serve as a background for the pieced blocks are made of white, red, and blue calico.

Verily Hopkins's cotton quilt Johnnie Round the Corner (Plate 44), pieced circa 1930, is from an old well-known traditional quilt pattern. And like most old patterns, over the years it has acquired several names such as Broken Wheel, Single Wedding Ring, Peek-A-Boo, and Wheel. Just like her Rooster Tails quilt, Verily Hopkins set the orange and white pieced blocks of her Johnnie Round the Corner quilt on point. Surrounded by an orange and white straight band border, quilted six or seven stitches per inch over a thin batting, Verily's quilt is still attractive despite being a well-used quilt exhibiting discernible signs of wear.

Obviously, the three quilts of Verily Hopkins in the collection were made as utilitarian bedcovers, as all of them showed signs of sustained use. Notwithstanding their age and worn condition, her quilts exude a certain charm. Verily Hopkins was apparently an experienced and skillful quiltmaker. Her red and white cotton Job's Tears quilt (Plate 45), made circa 1930, is another of her two-color quilts. In the center of each pieced block is a small red and white four-patch. Overall, the quilt blocks are sashed vertically and horizontally in red and white. At the corners where the sashings meet, Verily placed small red and white nine-patches. That kind of set, with nine patches at the corners, was a popular one in the early decades of the twentieth century. Her Job's Tears was quilted six or seven stitches per inch over a thin batting. It was hand quilted, but the biding was attached by machine.

Docella Johnson was from Bradley, Arkansas, and lived there until her death in the 1920s. She worked as a cook and general housekeeper for a white family, the McKinneys. For her quiltmaking Docella arranged a "halves" system with the McKinneys. The McKinney's mother provided the materials for two quilts and received one completed quilt in return. Docella kept the second quilt. Docella stopped working for the McKinney family about 1918.

The Buzz Saw (Plate 46), a pieced and appliquéd quilt, was made 1900–1920 by Docella Johnson in Bradley, Arkansas. Buzz Saw's nine large 21-inch square blocks are cream, pale orange, and wedgwood blue, separated by two-inch sashing of chrome orange. In the corners of each block are four small white appliquéd triangular-shaped motifs. Docella called these shapes "chicken feet," possibly another idiomatic term unique to rural Arkansas. What would be more familiar to a farm woman than the footprint of a chicken? Materials in the Buzz Saw quilt are hand-dyed cottons, sacking, and a little calico. It is quilted three to four stitches per inch over a medium batting.

In 1924 Beulah Smith of Paragould, Arkansas, pieced a similar, but not identical quilt to Docella Johnson's Buzz Saw quilt. Beulah Smith gave the name Rising Sun (Plate 47) to her quilt. While the block pattern of the Rising Sun is basically the same as the Buzz Saw, the block dimensions of 17-inch square for the Rising Sun are smaller than those of Docella Johnson's quilt (Plate 48, detail block of Rising Sun). There is no sashing on the sixteen-block Rising Sun quilt, nor does it contain the little motifs that Docella called "chicken feet." Placed on a background of medium blue, the wheel-shaped centers of the "sun" blocks are light and dark orange, encircled by green and dark-orange triangles. Bordered by an orange binding, Beulah's Rising Sun quilt has a thin batting quilted seven to eight stitches per inch. She intentionally made the Rising Sun quilt in colors of the sky, as it was meant to be a special quilt. Beulah made the quilt as a wedding gift to her employer.

Beginning in the 1920s, Beulah Smith was hired as a cook and helper to a white family in Paragould. Beulah's husband, William, worked at the same strip mining company as did her employer's husband, who held the position of foreman. Considered both a fine cook and an excellent seamstress, Beulah made many clothes and quilts for her employer's family. In the family's kitchen/multipurpose room were large quilting frames suspended from the ceiling that Beulah used for quilting. Though she made numerous quilts, the Rising Sun quilt is the only extant quilt of Beulah's work. Perhaps this quilt was preserved because it had been a special wedding gift from years ago. A descendant of the white family remembers a delicious treat that Beulah would make especially for him, a molasses cake cooked in a skillet. Beulah Smith died in the 1940s.

Time and again, in our research of African American quilts, not just in Arkansas but in many places, we have encountered situations similar to Beulah Smith's circumstances. Instances where the only known surviving quilt works of a black quiltmaker have been preserved by a white family for whom the quilter worked are common. Understandably, those black families living in poverty had a greater need to use their quilts continually until they were worn out. Certainly all black families were not poverty stricken, but in my investigations, I have encountered fewer middle-class black families who made quilts. This particularly holds true when searching for African American quilts made seventy-five years or more ago like the Beulah Smith Rising Sun quilt. So saying, I must clarify my observations. I am not stating that even one hundred years ago only poor blacks made quilts and that no middle-class blacks made quilts. My research revealed *more* impoverished blacks made quilts, and *fewer* middle-class blacks constructed quilts in the first decades of the century. A number of factors such as economics, family traditions, immediate environments, and an individual's own creative impulses were among the influences brought to bear on the presence or absence of quiltmaking in black households.

Five quilts in the collection made by Dorothy Lambert White, Conway, Arkansas, exemplify a current debate raging in the area of African American quilts studies. Beginning in the late 1970s until the present time, when African American quilts and their makers received substantial public notice, two interrelated questions have invariably surfaced. The two questions are (a) How can black-made quilts be distinguished from white-made quilts? and (b) How can one recognize a black-made quilt simply by viewing it? Considering the lengthy, complex, and involved history of African Americans and the great diversity of lifestyles and aesthetic sensibilities that exist within the large black segment of the American population, the questions appear to be simplistic and poorly conceived. Yet those questions, especially as they relate to African Americans, are characteristic of much of late twentieth-century America with its reliance on pop-culture–derived answers, quick sound-byte replies, and the unrealistic expectations that the most complicated topics require only casual observation and attention to solve. Upon examining Dorothy Lambert White's quilts the dichotomy of what she actually made, and why, and applying that omnipresent duo of questions to her works becomes readily apparent.

The Nursery Rhyme Figures quilt (Plate 49) made by Dorothy Lambert White, Conway, Arkansas, circa 1940, a fairly innocuous little embroidered child's quilt, will probably generate some controversy. There may be complaints from a number of viewers as they exclaim, "That is not an African American quilt!" If they mean that the black Arkansan quiltmaker Dorothy Lambert White did not originate the quilt's design, they will be correct. She did not design this quilt, nor did any of the other hundreds of quilters across the nation who made this same quilt. All of them purchased the transfer design sold by the pattern's manufacturer. The original Nursery Rhyme Figures quilt was designed by someone employed by the commercial company that manufactured the transfer pattern and distributed it nationally. It seems a reasonable assumption that Dorothy Lambert White saw and admired the pattern, purchased it, and made the quilt for her home. Why did Dorothy make the Nursery Rhyme Figures quilt? Perhaps like Herma Wilson Williams, whose quiltmaking was discussed earlier, simply because "she wanted to."

If the statement, "That is not an African American quilt," contains an implied criticism that the quilt does not exhibit certain ethnic characteristics many persons associate with African American quilts, is it not, in a larger sense, inferring that black people are a monolithic group who must adhere to a preordained and imposed aesthetic and are prohibited from exhibiting any diversity? In mounting the exhibition "A Piece of My Soul: Quilts by Black Arkansans," one of the Old State House Museum's objectives is to present *the true story* of the quilts made by black residents of Arkansas. If a black Arkansan quilter made a quilt the design of which was manufactured by a commercial entity, then the museum is unwilling to deny or hide that fact. Dorothy made the child's quilt fifty years ago, and in keeping with the title of the exhibition, that is sufficient reason to include her quilt in "A Piece of My Soul: Quilts by Black Arkansans."

Dorothy embroidered images of familiar nursery rhymes on twenty-eight white squares that alternated with plain pink squares. Like many old-time quilters, she hand quilted in pink thread straight through the embroidered blocks and the plain pink blocks without devising separate quilting designs for the alternating squares. The eight-inch blocks were machine stitched together, but the pink border was attached by hand stitching. Dorothy hand colored with crayons the embroidered squares, then set the crayon colors with a hot iron, a technique quite popular in the 1930s and 1940s.[10]

Dorothy Lambert White's Strip quilt (Plate 50), circa 1940, is a typical asymmetrically pieced, utilitarian bedcover. A two-sided quilt, pieced both front and back in a random fashion, the improvisational Strip quilt is made of six different cotton fabrics. Its binding is lapped over from back to front. Dorothy's Strip quilt does conform to several

Figure 6. The traditional Broken Dishes design.

Figure 7. A Broken Dishes variation.

of the criteria often used to identify African American quilts. It has large stitches and is quilted two to three stitches per inch over a thin batt. The quilt gives evidence of being well used.

What a mélange of colors comprise Dorothy Lambert White's circa 1950 *Broken Dishes* scrap quilt (Plate 51)! By incorporating innumerable little scraps of red, robin's egg blue, pink, white, black, yellow, orange, green, red-and-white stripe, black-and-white check, orange-and-white stripe with no intersecting sashing to define the sixty-three squares, one might think the quilt pattern's shape would disappear in this multitude of colors. Not so. Dorothy's employment of two versions of the Broken Dishes pattern, the familiar traditional one, and a second more complex version, helped to maintain the integrity of the pattern image on each square. She used both of the following versions of Broken Dishes on her quilt.

It was in the manipulation of colors in the second variation of Broken Dishes that Dorothy displayed her creativity. At times she placed a dominant color on a block's large triangles, perhaps a bright turquoise blue that made the paler colors on that same block recede. At other times, the small triangles contained the strongest color which gave the block an entirely different appearance. When Dorothy concentrated all of the blocks containing vibrant red patches right across the middle of her quilt, the center row became the focus of the quilt. Broken Dishes was quilted three stitches per inch over a medium batting. Its backing was lapped to the front for the binding.

Again on her Fly Foot and Nine Patch scrap quilt (Plate 52), Dorothy Lambert White utilized two separate quilt patterns to make the top. Whereas her Broken Dishes quilt consisted of two variants of the same pattern, her Fly Foot and Nine Patch quilt included two autonomous, distinctive unrelated quilt patterns. Her Nine Patch blocks were composed of small dark print and plain-pink four patches alternating with plain-pink patches. The Fly Foot design, also known as Whirligig, Pinwheel, or Swastika, is placed on a white, light-colored, or print fabric. Though the Fly Foot design and the Nine Patch design are unrelated as to structure, an overall view of Dorothy's quilt reveals a startling arrangement. She aligned the dark patches of the Nine Patch blocks to form diagonal "connections or paths" to the Fly Foot squares.

These paths or connections are so noticeable, it is difficult to assume Dorothy's arrangement of Fly Foot and Nine Patch was accidental or mere happenstance, or that she was unaware of what she was doing. Her entire quilt has these dark diagonals connecting to, even framing, the Fly Foot blocks. We are compelled to believe Dorothy's organizing of this quilt top was intentional because the arrangement of the dark paths is consistent throughout the quilt's surface. Other examples of her work indicate each quilt is different in construction and concept, and so she apparently was open to new ideas and wanted to try them out. Among black Arkansans, Dorothy represents the quintessential quilt experimenter. Obviously she was a person who was dissatisfied with repeating the same design endlessly.

The Fly Foot and Nine Patch cotton quilt is composed of twelve-inch squares and is quilted four stitches to the inch. Its pieced border is of print fabric. The fading plain-pink material has bled onto some of the dark patches and also seeped through to the quilt's backing. Otherwise, the quilt is in good condition.

A fifth quilt of Dorothy Lambert White's in the collection is the Friendship Star quilt (Plate 53), pieced circa 1940 in Conway, Arkansas. An eight-pointed star design with a circular open center, it is a traditional quilt pattern dating from the nineteenth century. An old custom was to have the quiltmaker's friends' signatures written on the open center of the star design, hence the name Friendship Star. Dorothy Lambert White's Friendship Star quilt has no signatures. Its thirty blocks, set in a traditional symmetrical manner, are separated by narrow blue sashing with small red squares at the corners where the vertical and horizontal sashings meet. The two outer borders of the Friendship Star are wider than the borders at the head and foot of the quilt. Like most of her other quilts, this, too, has a muslin back lapped to the front and was quilted five to six stitches per inch.

According to her great-granddaughter's statement, many of Leonia Taylor's quilts were dispersed over time throughout their family. Leonia Taylor's quilts had been made during the period of circa 1900 to the 1930s; none dates past the 1930s. The oldest quilt of Leonia's in the museum's collection is her red, tan, and white Star of Bethlehem (Plate 54), made circa 1900 as a wedding gift. Although created as a special presentation quilt, pragmatic-based decisions by Leonia went into the making of the Star of Bethlehem quilt. One of its borders is a single pieced strip of red and tan; the opposite border, also red and tan, is made of two strips. Family reports recount the reason for the difference in the construction of the borders. It was the desire not to waste fabric. The single strip border was to be placed on the side of the bed

Figure 8. A detail illustrating how some of the paths formed by the dark squares connect to the Fly Foot squares.

next to the wall, and the double strip border would be facing the room. Also at the top of the quilt is one-half of the pieced star design. Leonia planned that portion of the quilt to be hidden by pillows, and so there was no need to piece in a full-sized star block. Additionally, it would be easy to tell the top from the bottom of the quilt. Despite its age, the Star of Bethlehem quilt is in good condition and looks as if it received little actual use.

A handsome tan and gray Four Patch quilt (Plate 55) pieced by Leonia Taylor, circa 1920, is a fine example of a dramatic optical quilt. At first glance it appears to be a quilt with an overlay of broad, diagonally placed, gray stripping combined with a subtle background of tan-and-gray-print four patches. Or this "fool-the eye" quilt could be four patches set on point and sewn within the gray stripping that surrounds each block. Small triangles of pink with the same tonal values as the tan triangles, placed at the top and bottom of the quilt, are understated touches that add much to this illusory work.

The Spools quilt (Plate 56) attributed to Leonia Taylor seems a little out of character when compared to other quilts known to have been made by her. It lacks somewhat the earmarks of "the Leonia Taylor style." Yet we know a quilt's appearance can be affected by factors such as the purpose for which the quilt was made, the circumstances under which it was made, when it was made (we do not have even a circa date for Spools), the age of the quilter at the time of the quilt's making, and whether the quilt was a single-handed or a joint quiltmaking effort. Nevertheless, the dominant bright blue sashing coupled with the pale pastel pieced squares that create the impression of being background blocks do comply with the Leonia Taylor style. Pieced on thirty-six squares the Spools design, occasionally called the Arkansas Traveler, is an easily constructed pattern. Relatives have noted that Leonia did not like to work with tiny pieces for her quilts, and the Spools quilt requires only five sewn patches to complete a block. Notwithstanding any differences the Spools quilt may exhibit from other Leonia Taylor quilts, the family's attribution of the quiltmaker's identity should stand as reported.

Even if we did not have a date for Leonia's Fancy Dresden Plate quilt (Plate 57), the ubiquitous pattern itself, the purple sashing, the uniform yellow circular centers applied to the pastel fabric scraps would provide clues as to the date of its origin. For this quilt the family of Leonia supplied a date of 1920s-1930s. The Dresden Plate design was pervasive in the early decades of the twentieth century. It and the Double Wedding Ring, the Butterfly, the Sunbonnet Sue, and the Grandmother's Flower Garden were quilt patterns offered from a myriad of sources, as paper patterns in newspapers, in magazines, as ready-made cloth kits, as free premiums connected to merchandise sales.[12] Competitive events such as state and county fairs of the1930s were often innundated with examples of quilts made in these five favorite patterns. Leonia pieced and appliquéd a multitude of varicolored print and plain scraps for her twenty-block Fancy Dresden Plate quilt. Her quilting and embroidery designate this quilt as a special piece, a fact also borne out by the family.

Needlewoman Lula Bradford James, Dodderidge, Arkansas, was born in 1917 or 1918. Both of her parents died in the influenza epidemic of 1918–1919 when she was an infant. A couple named Fields raised Lula. When she was in her middle teens, Lula married Pete James and one child, a daughter Katie, was born to the couple in 1934. Lula became an excellent seamstress who not only quilted, but also did lovely crochet, embroidery, and tatting. Lula Bradford James took great pride in her ability to create beautiful items with her needle. She taught her daughter Katie needlework skills, too. When Katie was in her late teens, her father, Pete James, who worked for the railroad, was killed in an accident at his job. Later Katie married "Pee Wee" Beck and moved her mother, Lula, to Louisiana shortly thereafter. Lula Bradford James resumed quilting in her new home. Katie said her mother made dozens, if not hundreds of quilts during her lifetime and gave most of them away. Lula died of cancer in the late 1980s.

One of the most imaginatively conceived quilts of a genre of quilts in vogue in the 1930s to 1950s is Lula Bradford James's Contained Crazy quilt (Plate 58), made circa 1950. In America crazy quilt making became a fad in the last quarter of the nineteenth century. Those crazy quilts were made of irregular shaped and sized patches of silks, satins, brocades, velvets, and taffetas, heavily embellished with numerous fancy embroidery stitches, painted pictures, ribbons, and inscriptions.[13] Although the fashion for the ornately decorated silk crazy quilts had waned by the first decade of the twentieth century, quiltmakers continued to produce crazy quilts, albeit in a less elaborate form. Early twentieth-century quilts made in the crazy-patch style had far less or even, at times, no embroidery on the seams and were made of print or plain cotton or of lightweight wool as utility, rather than ornamental quilts. Revived about 1930 was the crazy quilt formulated in yet another fabrication scheme. This third reincarnation of the crazy quilt fad utilized a large collection of men's neckties. This third fad imposed a specification that was not necessary when making the previous two types of crazy quilts. It was essential regardless to whatever cutting of the tie fabric was required, that enough of the original shape of the necktie be maintained to be recognizable as a tie.[14] If the tie image could not be readily identified, one had just not made a real necktie crazy quilt.

Lula Bradford James's Contained Crazy quilt is unique as each block contains a miniature crazy quilt made of men's neckties placed to radiate out from the center of each square. She placed a small embroidered dark square at the center of each block to cover where the tops of the neckties meet. Running down the middle of her red satin sashing is a narrow dark strip. Compared to other necktie crazy quilts, Lula's quilt is much more orderly and neater than most. Katie said she obtained the red satin, the black satin, and the silk neckties from the family for whom her husband, Pee Wee, worked. Katie gave the materials to her mother.

Lula Bradford James's Flower Basket quilt (Plate 59) was pieced circa 1930, prior to the making of her Contained Crazy quilt. But even twenty years earlier, when making the Flower Basket, Lula's creativity was evident. Although the Flower Basket is old and worn from much use, one can still see how she used ruching to frame each block. Ruching is a technique most often reserved for making flowers on floral quilt designs. I have never seen ruching used as a sashing all over a quilt. Lula's quilt has been laundered frequently, and its colors have faded, but even so, one can tell this was a spectacular quilt when it was newly made. The Flower Basket is oddly sized and may appear to be a cut-down quilt, but close inspection of the quilt reveals these unusual dimensions were almost certainly its original ones.

An example of the "waste not, want not" philosophy is embodied in Lula Bradford James's Salesman Sample quilt (Plate 60), made in the 1940s–1950s era. The fabrics were samples of wool suiting materials. Several of the pieces on the quilt show small holes near one end. These holes were where the pieces fit over the rings of the sample book. Earlier specimens of salesman samples were often glued to pasteboard cards. Lula's Salesman Sample quilt was made as a bedspread and did not have a heavy cotton filling. Pieced as a strip quilt, the strips are an even, uniform size although the colors are randomly placed. Just as her

Contained Crazy quilt has a neat look, so does her Salesman Sample strip quilt.

Though Lula Bradford James pieced the Broken Star quilt with a zigzag border (Plate 61) in the late 1930s, the top was not quilted until the early 1980s by her daughter, Katie. Its subdued soft color combinations on both the central star and border designs contrast sharply with the strong, vivid primary colors often seen on versions of the Broken Star or the pastel ones so common in the 1930s when Lula made her quilt. Her zigzag border forms the perfect frame for this design. Katie said her mother pieced far more tops than she ever quilted, and when she died, Lula left some completed tops that needed only quilting. Over the years, Katie has quilted several of her mother's tops. Lula Bradford James was an accomplished quiltmaker who added her own original ideas to the classic quilt patterns she made.

Beatrice Ruth Calhoun Williamson (called Ruth by the family) was born and lived most of her life in Texarkana. She married William Wiliamson in 1910. Their first child, a son, died in the influenza epidemic in 1917. A daughter, Maxine, was born in 1919. Maxine grew up, married Woodrow Wilson, and moved to Hot Springs, Arkansas. Maxine Wilson, who presently lives in Dallas, Texas, owned the quilts made by her late mother, Ruth.

The Donkey quilt (Plate 62) was pieced by Beatrice Ruth Calhoun Williamson, Texarkana, in 1932–1934. The Donkey quilt pattern first appeared in the *Kansas City Star* in 1931. A few weeks earlier the newspaper had published the pattern of "Ararat," an elephant in Swope Park, a Kansas City, Missouri, zoo. Interpreting the political significance of the elephant as a Republican Party symbol, some readers made a GOP (Grand Old Party) elephant out of the pattern. To be even-handed, and in view of the upcoming presidential election of 1932, the readers wanted a donkey pattern to represent the Democrat Party. The *Kansas City Star* obliged them and published "Giddap, A Very Democratic Donkey," designed by Eveline Foland. The *Kansas City Star* was circulated throughout Arkansas in the *Weekly Star Arkansas/Oklahoma Edition,* as well as in some other states contiguous to Missouri, and so the Donkey quilt pattern was widely available to Arkansas residents such as Ruth.[14]

For black people, the Donkey pattern had a special meaning dictated by the Great Depression the country was experiencing and by the 1932 election of the Democrat Party candidate for president. Ever since the Republican president Abraham Lincoln issued the Emancipation

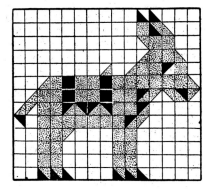

Figure 10. Giddap, A Very Democratic Donkey, quilt pattern designed by Eveline Foland, published in the *Kansas City Star,* July 22, 1931.

Proclamation in 1863 freeing the slaves in areas in rebellion against the Union, black people had a strong loyalty to the Republican Party. Once Amendment XV to the U.S. Constitution was passed in 1870 granting suffrage to black men, and in 1920 when Amendment XIX granted suffrage to all women citizens, from those times forward until 1932, black people almost overwhelmingly voted solidly Republican. Rather than to paint too rosy a picture of relations between Republicans and black voters, there were instances, especially in some southern areas in the early twentieth century, when Republicans attempted to and succeeded to disenfranchise black voters. And the GOP also resisted a prevailing impression that somehow blacks were too influential in the party by increasingly separating white and black party members and by sponsoring segregation legislation of its own. Yet, by and large, most blacks during that period favored the Republican Party over the Democrat Party.

From the end of the Civil War to first three decades of the twentieth century the Democrat Party, dominated by zealous southern segregationists, was generally considered an anathema to black voters. Many believed the Democrat Party firmly upheld the southern way of life with all of its ills that negatively affected black people in every aspect of their lives, socially, politically, economically, educationally, and culturally. Legal "Jim Crow" segregation laws initiated and supported by the Democrat Party produced a climate of fear, suppression, isolation, and overt racism and were the bane of black people's existence. In such an atmosphere brutal lynchings, sharecropper peonage, and deprivation of educational opportunities for blacks flourished.

When Franklin D. Roosevelt, a Democrat, became president, he soon set about combating the Great Depression in which millions of desperate Americans were jobless by instituting government measures and programs, such as the WPA (Works Progress Administration), and its agencies, the CCC, the TVA, the FWP, and a number of others. For the first time blacks were allowed to participate, although many of the programs were poorly administered, so black participation was uneven at best. President Roosevelt's wife, Eleanor, who was enlightened on social issues, began to be perceived as an advocate for the poor and for blacks. Gradually more and more blacks began to switch their allegiance from the Republican Party to the Democrat Party in the name of self-interest.

Thus it seems that black Arkansan Ruth Williamson was making a political statement when she pieced the Donkey quilt, the symbol of the Democrat Party. Further evidence to support that theory is that her quilt was made in the patriotic colors of the United States, red, white, and blue, instead of the colors suggested of brown, white, and orange on the original published pattern of the *Kansas City Star.*

Jessie Jones was born in Monticello, Arkansas, in 1923, the only daughter in a family of six. She married at the age of sixteen and had five children. Her husband worked whenever he could, and they moved around Arkansas quite a bit before finally settling in Shreveport, Louisiana, in the early 1980s. Jessie's mother and grandmother taught her to quilt. They quilted frequently with other female family members, and Jessie said, "We made some of the prettiest strip quilts you ever did see." Jessie's mother liked to piece all kinds of quilts, but she always liked the strip quilts best. They would buy bundles of remnants and combine them with feed sacks and the good pieces of old clothes to make quilt tops. They made many "britches quilts" from the good sections of worn-out overalls and pants. Quilting was done on frames suspended from the ceiling in the main room of their three-room house. Jessie still pieces occasionally, but no longer quilts due to arthritis. All of her quilts are tied now, not quilted.

Jessie Jones's two-sided Strip quilt (Plate 63) was made in the mid-1960s in Crossett, Arkansas. Both sides of the utility quilt are pieced with multicolored fabrics of cotton, cotton flannel, denim, polyester, and wool. Placed in a "hit or miss" fashion are the predominantly rectangular-shaped patches. The improvisational quilt is tacked with navy-blue yarn, not quilted. Inside for filling is another old quilt.

Turkey Tracks variation quilt (Plate 64) was made by Sally Epps, Taylor, Arkansas, in the late 1930s. Sally Epps is deceased. A close friend who knew Sally in her later years reported on her prolific quiltmaking. Sally was particularly fond of bright color combinations in her quilts and especially favored orange. Her Turkey Tracks variation quilt is a mixture of improvisational and traditional piecing. On some blocks, the pattern is readily detected; on others the pattern seems to have lost its structure within the block. Yet the overall size and configuration of the blocks, which are basically enlarged hexagons, do not vary. Around the outer edges of the quilts, on all four sides, Sally placed half blocks, but again she improvised. She also placed partial portions of the blocks along the edges as well. This vibrant orange and red quilt is bordered with yellow and brown strips. It is quilted four stitches per inch.

Dallie Head was born in Dodderidge, Arkansas, in 1898 and died in Shreveport, Louisiana, in 1990. Dallie's Medallion quilt (Plate 65) was made in the late 1930s or early 1940s in Dodderidge. Framed by a black and white striped material, the center medallion is of a floral print material topped by a smaller element of bright red and peach. An outstanding feature of Dallie's Medallion quilt is balance. On either side of her framed medallion, Dallie placed two vertical strips of the same black and white material used for the frame. Below the medallion, she pieced two horizontal strips that run across the quilt full length. Those two strips are of the black-and-white and brown-and-white-striped fabric. At the top of the quilt, again using the black and white and brown and white striped material in a horizontal strip running full length across the quilt, she interspersed at intervals patches of a plaid taffeta. The overall structure of planned balance gives Dallie Head's Medallion quilt a pleasing look.

Jessie Lee Jones, quiltmaker, married Sam Jones, and the couple had ten children, eight of whom lived to adulthood. Sam and Jessie Lee were farm workers and sharecroppers on several cotton farms in the northern Louisiana, Caddo, and Shreveport areas. Jessie Lee was an ardent Baptist, looked forward to her church activities, and sang in the choir. Jessie Lee quilted all of her life for cover, using sewing scraps and things people would give to her. Jessie Lee learned to quilt from her mother, who had been taught to quilt by her mother, and so there was a three-generation tradition of quilting in Jessie Lee's family. They saved and used many feed sacks for the backings of their quilts. Sometimes they quilted with the thread they unraveled and saved from the feed sacks.

Jessie Lee Jones's Log Cabin variation quilt (Plate 66) was made in 1967. The thirty-block quilt is made up of many different colors, fabrics, and styles, such as cotton, silk, polyester double knits, and even a few patches of taffeta. A brown and gray striped material as well as a rust multiprint comprise the pieced backing. Over a medium batting, the Log Cabin variation is quilted two stitches per inch. The quilt is in excellent, like-new condition.

When Mae Thompson's Unknown quilt (Plate 67) was located, unfortunately no information about the quilt or its maker was found. It is an intriguing quilt, and further research is anticipated. The quilt's deep coloration of navy blue, hot pink, and orange coupled with the unusual quilt design places this piece in a mystery-to-be-solved category. So investigations of both the quilt itself and a genealogical search for information about the quiltmaker are forthcoming.

Several quilts in the Old State House Museum's collection were made by black Arkansans whose names are unknown to us. One circa 1930 cotton quilt is from the Little Rock area. It has alternating blocks of Nine Patch and Rolling Stone patterns (Plate 68). Most of the Nine Patch blocks are made in various patterned fabrics, while the Rolling Stone squares are primarily plain pink, green, and white. The quiltmaker put an unexpected touch to her quilt. Whereas the Nine Patch squares alternate with the Rolling Stone squares over the body of the quilt, the last two rows do not alternate in this manner. Rather two rows of Nine Patch blocks are side by side with no Rolling Stone blocks to be seen. It gives the quilt a bit of a zing, a little surprise. The Nine Patch–Rolling Stone is a recovered quilt. Inside is an old circa 1900 or before Eight-Pointed Star quilt which makes a very thick batting. The Nine Patch and Rolling Stone is tacked with red yarn ties. The binding, a rayon print material, was brought from the back to the front. As the quilt is not in good condition, we believe it was well used.

Another anonymous quilt, the Central Medallion (Plate 69), circa 1970, was made of satin ribbon strips. It does not have batting, nor is it quilted. Some persons may think of the Central Medallion as a summer spread or perhaps just a quilt top. If a quilt top, it would seem to indicate the piece is incomplete and needs quilting. We believe it is complete and was never meant to be quilted. We think it may have been made as a funeral cover. Made of polyester satin, the red, pink, yellow, and white Central Medallion cover is machine stitched. Other than some fading of the reds, its condition is good. In rural black communities while homemade coffin covers are not plentiful household items, they are not uncommon. Coffin covers are frequently made of silk, satin, and taffeta ribbons, and because they are used only occasionally and temporarily, they can last a long time. Funeral covers are removed prior to burial of the deceased and can be handed down for several generations in a family. Persons have been known to collect the ribbons and bows that decorate floral funeral wreaths, take them home, and iron them to add to their cache in preparation for making coffin covers. Because the satin Central Medallion cover was pieced by an unknown maker, we cannot state definitively the cover is a funeral piece.

The Strip Quilt (Plate 70), made in 1920–1930, is still another quilt by an unknown maker. The Strip quilt was found in the Cotton Plant, Arkansas, area. It has all of the characteristics of an old-fashioned "use up the pieces" strip quilt—varying width and length of the strips, a multitude of print and plain materials, and a thick batting with seeds in it. There are knots on the top. The backing is home-dyed fabric and faded feed-sack material. Still visible on the backing is some of the printing:

> Feeding Instructions
>
> Will grow and fatten hogs fast.
> Furnish plenty of fresh ———
> It is possible to make 2 lb. of pork
> with 3–4 lbs. of sh——

The Strip quilt featured here is in very good condition and is quilted two to four stitches per inch.

The Double Pyramid quilt (Plate 71), circa 1950, maker unknown, found in Cotton Plant is a twenty-five-block cotton quilt. Its colors are mainly browns, with some reds and pinks. On the outer edge of the quilt is a row of very light-colored blocks with a floral sashing totally different from the blocks in the body of the quilt. It looks as if the maker may have wanted to enlarge the quilt and no longer had any of the materials used in the main body of the quilt. Several of the blocks do not follow the structure of the pattern. The Double Pyramid's blocks are approximately 11 inches, and has a thin batting that is quilted four stitches per inch. The quilt has a little deterioration but has been neatly patched. Otherwise its condition is good.

Scores of prints make up the String Diamonds quilt (Plate 72) pieced 1920–1930 by an unnamed black Arkansan quiltmaker. Within each large diamond, multicolored cotton scraps have been sewn like miniature crazy quilts. The String Diamonds is machine stitched and quilted. Though the quilt's condition is just fair, frayed a bit on the edges and some tears on the strips, it is a lively, cheerful-looking quilt because of the mass of bright-colored prints framed by the medium-green border.

Miniature Quilts

In recent years a new trend in quiltmaking has developed; the making of miniature quilts has gained favor with quilters nationwide. Patterns, books, and magazines solely devoted to miniature quilts have been published. Miniature quilt exhibitions have been mounted at a number of venues. Some people may mistake miniature quilts for doll quilts because of their small size, but doll quilts and miniature quilts are not the same. Because miniature quilts are replications of full-sized quilts, their making requires specific skills, including the ability to work effectively with tiny pieces and an acute sense of proportion.[16]

Gloria Scott, a black Arkansan quiltmaker, was originally from Hot Springs. Because of her husband's job transfer, she moved to the Greater Kansas City, Missouri, area in the early 1980s. She joined the main quilt guild in Kansas City and also a smaller offshoot quilt group. She met Sandra Todaro in both of the organizations and they became friends, partially because, they believe, of their mutual southern backgrounds, and certainly because of their mutual love of quilts. Gloria Scott began to make miniature quilts. She said by making miniatures she might be able to make all the patterns she wanted to make, whereas if she restricted herself to full-sized pieces, she would never be able to make that many quilts. All of Gloria's miniatures were handmade, some using vintage fabrics she salvaged from old quilt blocks. Two of the pieces have vintage fabrics in them; the Grandmother's Fan and the Churn Dash. Sandra Todaro admired Gloria Scott's skill and sense of color and proportion and bought the following seven miniatures from her. Later, Sandra and her husband, Joe Todaro, knowing of the Old State House Museum's project of collecting quilts made by black Arkansans, donated Gloria Scott's miniatures to the collection. The Todaros believed that Hot Springs native Gloria Scott's works would add another dimension to the museum's collection. All of the miniatures were made in 1984–1985. They are the Churn Dash, a very old classic pattern made with vintage fabrics (Plate 73); the Grandmother's Fan, an old pattern made with vintage fabrics (Plate 74); the Four Patch of Hearts, a modern pattern (Plate 75); the Diamond in a Square, an Amish-style quilt (Plate 76); the Roman Stripes, an Amish-style quilt (Plate 77); the Bars, an Amish-style quilt (Plate 78); and the Irish Chain, a very old classic pattern (Plate 79).

Black quiltmakers in Arkansas have left a rich cultural legacy for their state. Quiltmaking represented a unique opportunity for these rural black women to do two things at once; to provide nurture and care for their families, and to express themselves creatively. As Elaine Hedges wrote:

> Furthermore, we know from the records women left and from extant quilts, many in mint condition, that women created more of them than necessity demanded. Quilts became a vehicle through which women could express themselves; utilitarian objects elevated through enterprise, imagination and love to the status of an original art form.[17]

Moreover, examinations of the quilts of these black Arkansans revealed family histories, family lineages, customs, and morés. Those studies made it possible to reconstruct, to a degree, rural black Arkansans' environments and living conditions from the turn of the century to the present. The quilts themselves exhibited commonalities shared by the black communities, and diversities that celebrated individual creativity. Preservation of this body of black Arkansans' works is a laudable endeavor and will provide a rich resource for future scholarship.

Where the Quilters Lived in Arkansas

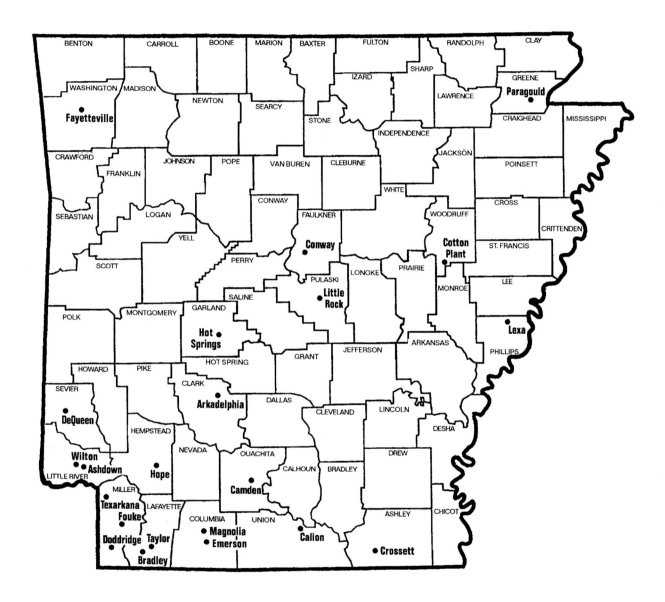

Figure 10. The quiltmakers cited lived in rural regions of mid-state and southern Arkansas. Very few quilts in the Old State House Museum's collection originated in the state's urban areas.

Quilters and Their Towns

Ashdown
Mary Harris

Arkadelphia
Hattie Collins*

Bradley
Docella Johnson*

Calion
Frances S. Wilson*
Minnie Ola Wilson Leary*
Authorine Wilson Anderson*
Eldora Wilson Thomas*
Welthia Wilson Wardlaw*

Camden
Mary Allen Williams*
Cordelia Allen Green*
Asia Cummings Shed*
Malsie Shed Bennett*
Myrtle Bennett*
Tillie Rae Williams Hall
Hattie Williams Jones

Columbia
Sally Epps*

Conway
Dorothy Lambert White*

Cotton Plant
Anonymous quilter*

Crossett
Jessie Jones*

De Queen
Verily Hopkins*

Dodderidge
Dallie Head*
Lula Bradford James*

Emerson
Sally Anna Ingram Parker*
Catherine Parker Hall*
Oscar Evans*

Fayetteville
The Modern Priscillas club

Garland County
Dorothy Hunter
Frances L. Polk

Hope
Lillie Mae Smith
Dessie Lee Benton

Hot Springs
Gloria Scott*
Justine C. Ross
Zeola Hale
Tracy Hale
Katie Williams

Lexa
Arkansas Country Quilts

Little Rock
Anonymous quilter*

Magnolia
Herma Wilson Williams*
Essie Jackson*
Alice Trammell

Paragould
Beulah Smith*

Taylor
Sally Epps*

Texarkana
Beatrice Ruth Calhoun Williamson*

Wilton
Zeola Geiger

Arkansas
(town, county unknown)
Mae Thompson*
Leonia Taylor*

* Black Arkansans whose quilts are in the collection of the Old State House Museum, Little Rock, Arkansas.

Other black Arkansans names listed made quilts that are presently in private collections and in the Michigan State University Museum, East Lansing, Michigan, collections.

Plate 1. Texas Star Quilt, made by Cordelia Allen Green, Camden, Arkansas, circa 1920, 71 x 70 inches, cotton, pieced. Purchase. Collection of Old State House Museum. 95.01.21.

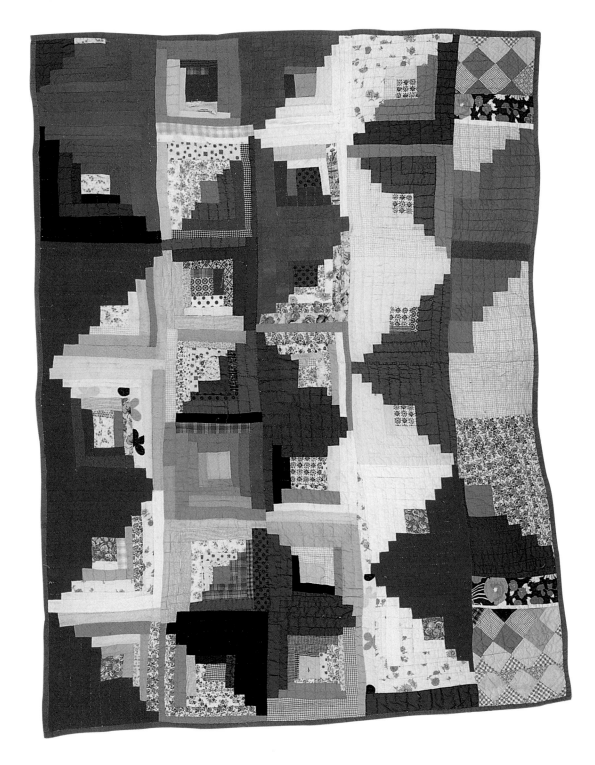

Plate 2. Log Cabin Quilt, made by Cordelia Allen Green, Camden, Arkansas, circa 1940, 87 x 64 inches, cotton, pieced. Purchase. Collection of Old State House Museum. 95.01.22.

Plate 3. Pine Cone Quilt, made by Mary Allen Williams, Camden, Arkansas, circa 1950, cut into two pieces: section A, 42 x 37 inches; section B, 42 x 37 inches, cotton, pieced. Purchase. Collection of Old State House Museum. 95.01.05 A&B.

Plate 4. Diamonds Quilt, made by Mary Allen Williams, Camden, Arkansas, circa 1950, 84 x 67 inches, cotton, pieced. Purchase. Collection of Old State House Museum. 95.01.1.

The Quilts

Plate 5. Center Medallion Quilt, made by Mary Allen Williams, Camden,
Arkansas, circa 1950, 77 x 68 1/4 inches, cotton, pieced. Purchase. Collection of
Old State House Museum. 95.01.2.

Plate 6. Log Cabin Quilt Variation, made by Mary Allen Williams, Camden, Arkansas, circa 1950, 77 5/8 x 65 1/2 inches, cotton, pieced. Purchase. Collection of Old State House Museum. 95.01.3.

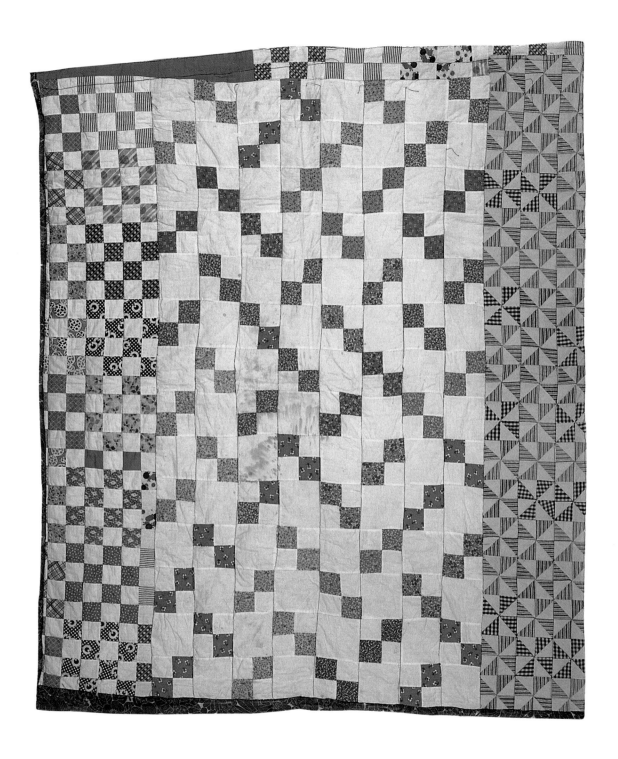

Plate 7. Pinwheel and Sixteen Patch Quilt, a recovered quilt made by Mary Allen
Williams, Camden, Arkansas, circa 1940; recovered by Hattie Williams Jones,
Fouke, Arkansas, circa 1960, 76 x 65 1/2 inches, cotton, pieced. Purchase.
Collection of Old State House Museum. 95.01.4.

Plate 8. Triangle Strip Quilt, made by Mary Allen Williams, Camden, Arkansas, circa 1960, 77 x 62 inches, cotton, rayon, polyester, pieced. Purchase. Collection of Old State House Museum. 95.01.6.

The Quilts

Plate 9. Medallion, Log Cabin Variation Quilt (it is also called Pig Pen in many areas of the South), made by Mary Allen Williams, Camden, Arkansas, circa 1920–1940, 82 x 73 inches, wool flannel, cotton, pieced. Purchase. Collection of Old State House Museum. 95.01.7.

Plate 10. Log Cabin Doll Quilt, made by Mary Allen Williams, Camden, Arkansas, circa 1940, 22 3/4 x 15 inches, cotton, pieced. Purchase. Collection of Old State House Museum. 95.01.9.

Plate 11. Slashed Album Strip Quilt, made by Mary Allen Williams, Camden, Arkansas, circa 1960, 63 x 63 1/4 inches, cotton, pieced. Purchase. Collection of Old State House Museum. 95.01.10.

Plate 12. Snowflake Quilt, made by Hattie Williams Jones, Fouke, Arkansas, circa 1945–1960, 89 x 76 inches, cotton, pieced. Purchase. Collection of Old State House Museum. 95.01.8.

Plate 13. Flyfoot or Brunswick Star or Jumping Jack Quilt, made by Hattie
Williams Jones for two of her sisters, Fouke, Arkansas, circa 1950, 92 x 82 inches,
cotton, machine pieced. Purchase. Collection of Old State House Museum.
95.01.11.

Plate 14. Flower Garden Quilt, made by Hattie Williams Jones, Fouke, Arkansas, circa 1970, 93 x 72 1/4 inches, polyester knit, cotton, pieced. Purchase. Collection of Old State House Museum. 95.01.13.

The Quilts

Plate 15. Star of Bethlehem Quilt, made by Hattie Williams Jones, Fouke,
Arkansas, circa, 1970, 80 x 49 inches, cotton, pieced. Purchase. Collection of Old
State House Museum. 95.01.14.

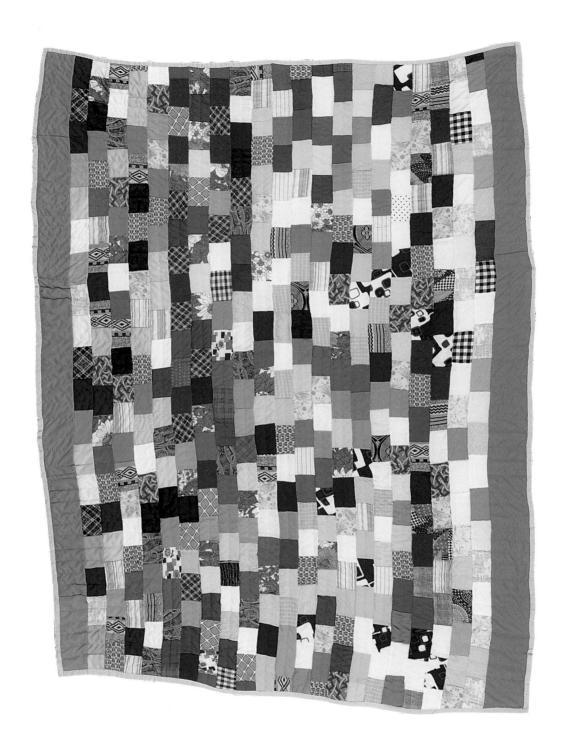

Plate 16. Brick Quilt, made by Hattie Williams Jones, Fouke, Arkansas, 1975, 82 x
66 1/4 inches, polyester double knits, pieced. Purchase. Collection of Old State
House Museum. 95.01.17.

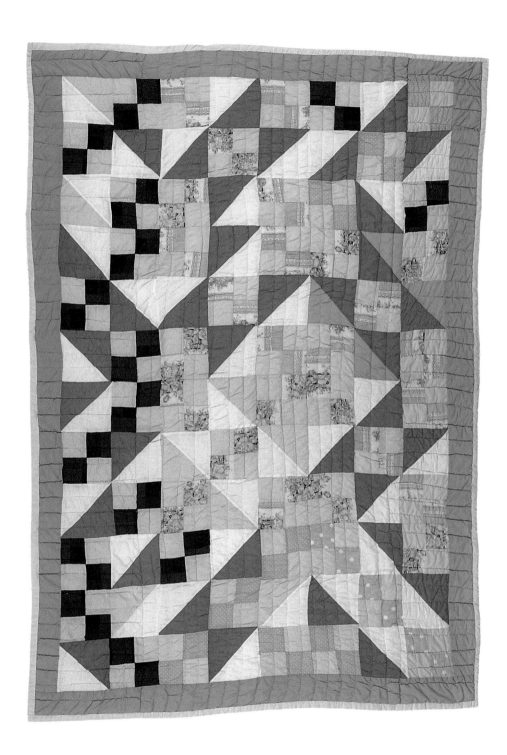

Plate 17. Jacob's Ladder and Sixteen Patch Quilt, made by Hattie Williams Jones, Fouke, Arkansas, 1986, 83 1/2 x 57 inches, cotton, polyester double knits, pieced. Purchase. Collection of Old State House Museum. 95.01.18.

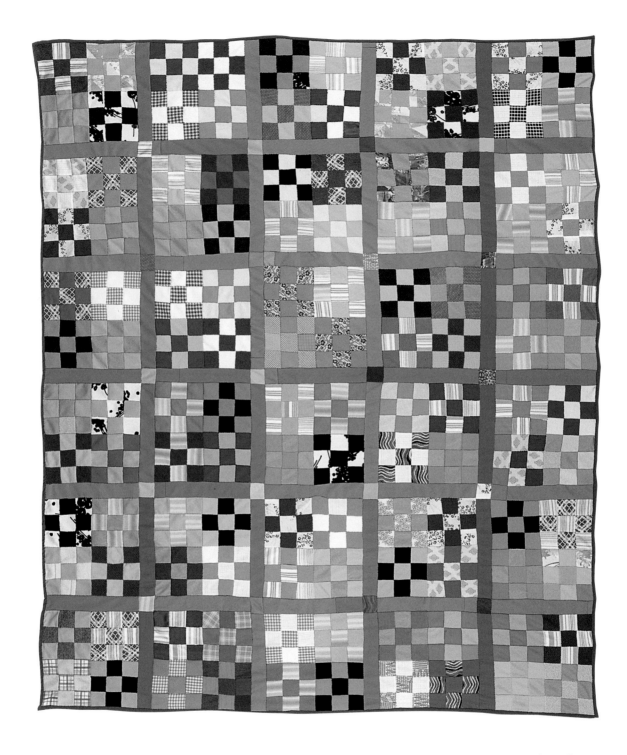

Plate 18. Knit Nine Patch Quilt, made by Hattie Williams Jones, Fouke, Arkansas, circa 1980, 94 x 77 inches, polyester double knits, pieced. Purchase. Collection of Old State House Museum. 95.01.23.

The Quilts

Plate 19. Log Cabin Quilt in courthouse-steps configuration, made by Tillie Rae
Williams Hall and twin sister, Willie Mae Williams Smith, Camden, Arkansas,
circa mid-1930s, 81 x 74 3/4 inches, seersucker, gingham, flannel, upholstery fabric,
tacked with red yarn, pieced. Purchase. Collection of Old State House Museum.
95.01.19.

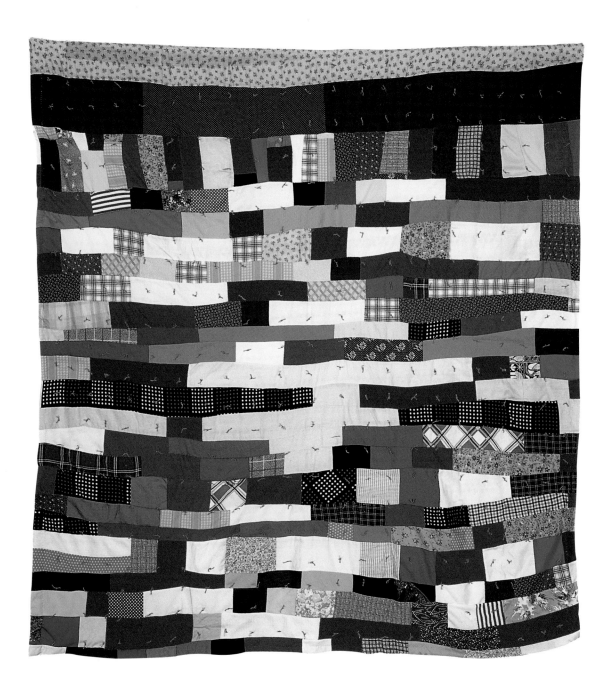

Plate 20. Lazy Gal Strip Quilt, made by Tillie Rae Williams Hall and Willie Mae Williams Smith, Camden, Arkansas, circa 1970, 83 1/2 x 79 inches, polyester double knits, tacked with green embroidery floss, pieced. Purchase. Collection of Old State House Museum. 95.01.15.

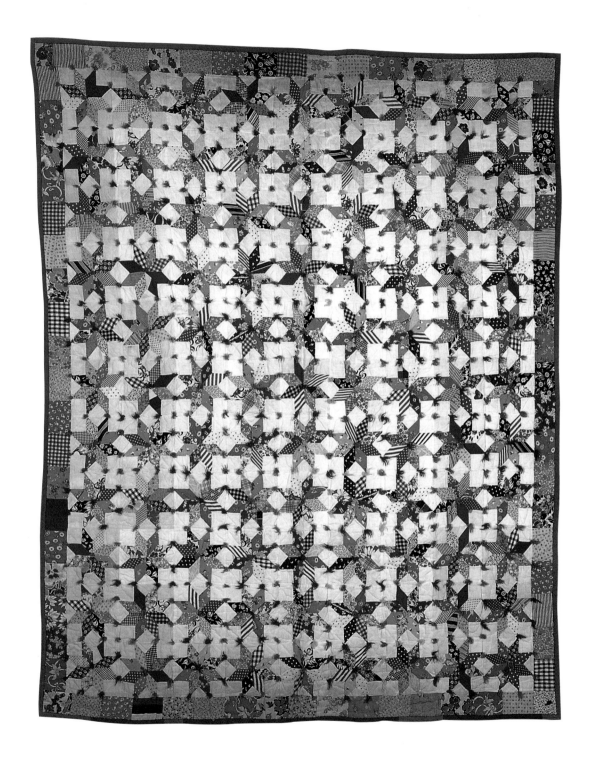

Plate 21. Lemon Star or Star of Lemoyne Quilt, made by Frances Smith Wilson,
Calion, Arkansas, circa mid-1930s, cotton, pieced. Purchase. Collection of Old
State House Museum. 96.01.4.

Plate 22. Butterfly Quilt, made by Authorine Wilson Anderson, Calion, Arkansas, circa 1930, cotton, appliquéd. Purchase. Collection of Old State House Museum. 96.01.7.

Plate 23. Boxed Star Quilt, made by Eldora Wilson Thomas, Calion, Arkansas,
circa mid-1960s, cotton, pieced. Purchase. Collection of Old State House
Museum. 96.01.1.

Plate 24. Pinwheel Quilt, made by Minnie Ola Wilson Leary, Calion, Arkansas, circa 1960, cotton, pieced. This piece is actually a summer spread as it has no batting between layers. Purchase. Collection of Old State House Museum. 96.01.06.

Plate 25. Central Medallion Quilt, made by Welthia Wilson Wardlaw, Calion,
Arkansas, 1989, cotton, pieced. Purchase. Collection of Old State House Museum.
96.01.5.

Plate 26. Log Cabin Quilt, made by Hattie Collins, a former slave, Magnolia, Arkansas, circa 1890, 74 x 63 1/2 inches, cotton, pieced. Purchase. Collection of Old State House Museum. 88.17.3.

Plate 27. "H" Quilt, made by Herma Wilson Williams, Magnolia, Arkansas, circa
1930, 76 x 62 inches, cotton, pieced. Purchase. Collection of Old State House
Museum. 88.17.1.

Plate 28. American Tree Quilt, made by Herma Wilson Williams, Magnolia, Arkansas, circa 1940, 79 1/2 x 64 inches, cotton, pieced. Purchase. Collection of Old State House Museum. 88.17.6.

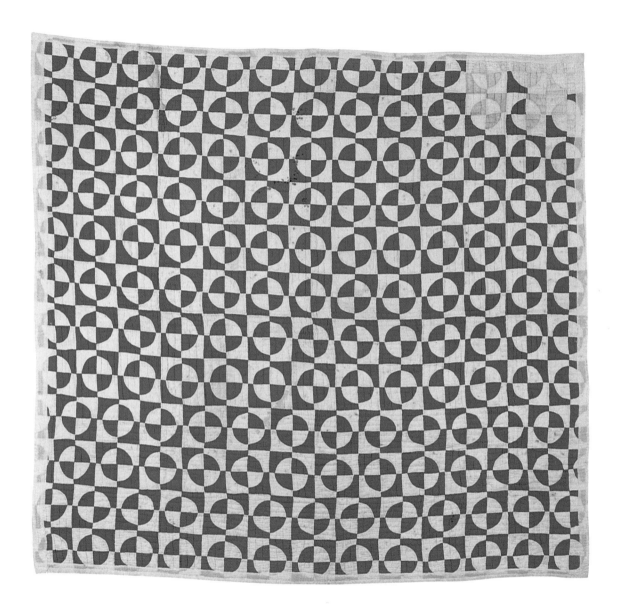

Plate 29. Snowball Quilt, made by Herma Wilson Williams, Magnolia, Arkansas, circa 1940, 75 x 69 1/2 inches, hand-bleached and dyed Bull Durham tobacco sacks, pieced. Purchase. Collection of Old State House Museum. 88.17.2.

Plate 30. Kite Quilt Block, made by Herma Wilson Williams, Magnolia, Arkansas, circa 1930, 13 1/2 x 7 1/2 inches, cotton, pieced. Pattern cut from front page of Marietta Daily Times ——y 24, 1930. Purchase. Collection of Old State House Museum. 88.17.12.

Plate 31. String quilt block and paper pattern, made by Herma Wilson Williams, Magnolia, Arkansas, circa 1930, cotton, pieced. Purchase. Collection of Old State House Museum. 88.17.11.

Plate 32. Dutch Tile Quilt, made by Essie Jackson, Magnolia, Arkansas, circa 1940,
90 x 72 1/4 inches, cotton, flannel, linen, grosgrain, pieced, and appliquéd.
Purchase. Collection of Old State House Museum. 88.17.5.

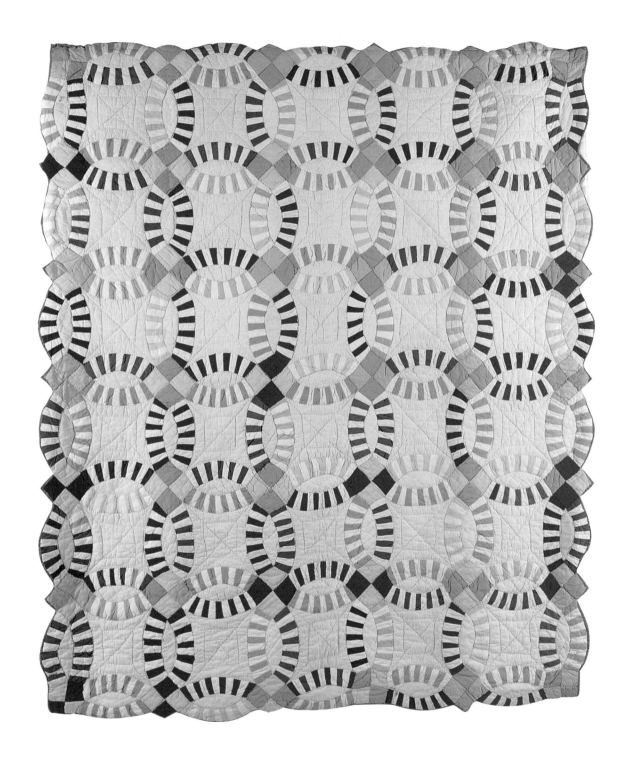

Plate 33. Double Wedding Ring Quilt, made by Essie Jackson, Magnolia, Arkansas, circa 1950, 85 x 69 1/2 inches, cotton, pieced. Purchase. Collection of Old State House Museum. 88.17.4.

Plate 34. Little Boy's Britches Quilt, made by Sally Anna Ingraham Parker, Haynesville, Arkansas, circa 1930, 78 1/2 x 66 inches, corduroy, cotton, pieced. Purchase. Collection of Old State House Museum. 95.01.25.

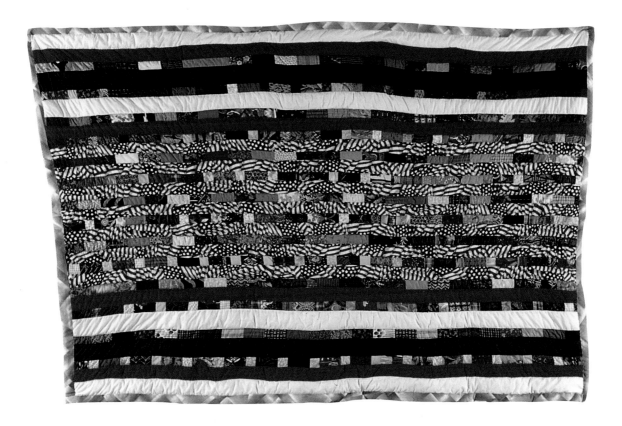

Plate 35. American Flag Quilt, made by Catherine Parker Hall, Emerson, Arkansas, circa 1990, 81–86 x 50 inches, cotton, pieced. Purchase. Collection of Old State House Museum. 95.01.24.

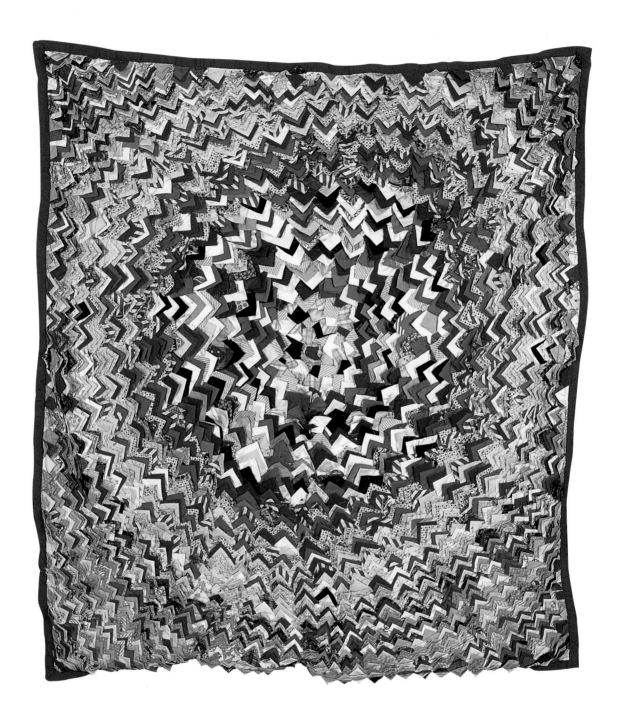

Plate 36. Pine Cone Quilt, made by Oscar Evans, Emerson, Arkansas, assisted by Catherine Parker Hall, 1986, cotton, rayon, pieced. Purchase. Collection of Old State House Museum. 96.01.3.

Plate 37. Stars Quilt, made by Asia Cummings Shed, Camden, Arkansas, circa
1890, cotton, pieced. Purchase. Collection of Old State House Museum. 96.01.14.

Plate 38. Lily Quilt, made by Asia Cummings Shed, Camden, Arkansas, circa 1890, cotton, pieced. Purchase. Collection of Old State House Museum. 96.01.15.

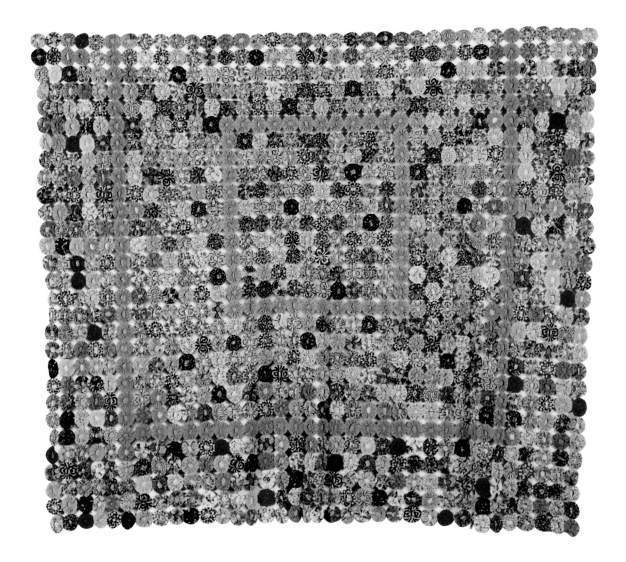

Plate 39. Yo-yo Quilt, made by Malsie Shed Bennett, Camden, Arkansas, circa 1920, cotton, pieced. A novelty type of construction that was made as a bedcover, but does not conform to the traditional definition of a three-layered quilt. Purchase. Collection of Old State House Museum. 96.01.12.

Plate 40. Yo-yo Quilt, a detail.

The Quilts

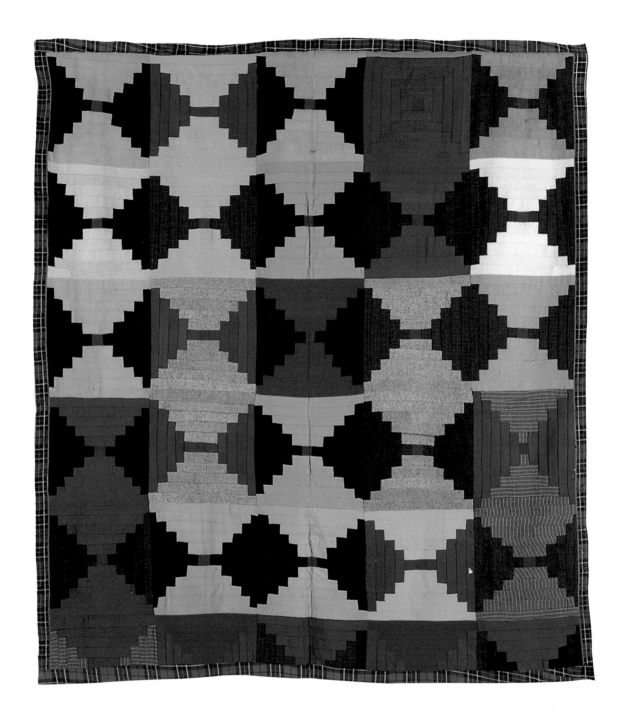

Plate 41. Log Cabin Quilt, made by Malsie Shed Bennett, Camden, Arkansas, 1975, suiting fabrics, and no batting, pieced. Collection of Old State House Museum. 96.01.13.

Plate 42. Trip Around the World Quilt, made by Malsie Shed Bennett, Camden, Arkansas, circa 1940, cotton, pieced. Purchase. Collection of Old State House Museum. 97.01.1.

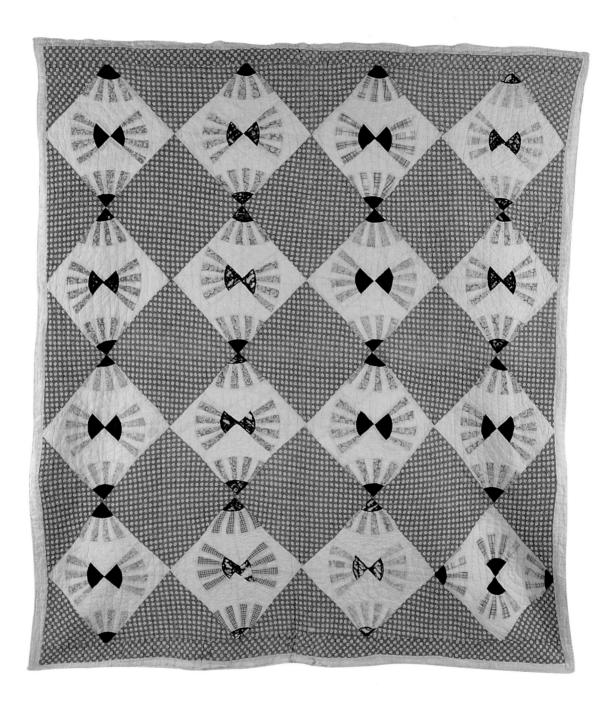

Plate 43. Rooster Tails or Grandmother's Fan Quilt, made by Verily Hopkins, DeQueen, Arkansas, circa 1930, 77 x 67 1/2 inches, cotton calicoes, pieced and appliquéd. Purchase. Collection of Old State House Museum. 88.40.3.

Plate 44. Johnnie Round the Corner Quilt, made by Verily Hopkins, DeQueen, Arkansas, circa 1930–1940, 77 x 67 inches, cotton, pieced. Purchase. Collection of Old State House Museum. 88.40.2.

The Quilts

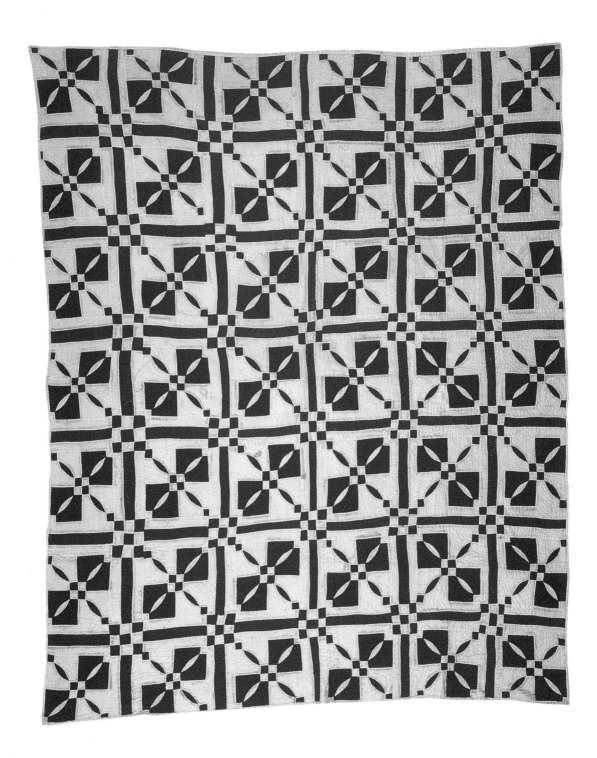

Plate 45. Job's Tears Quilt, made by Verily Hopkins, DeQueen, Arkansas, circa
1930–1940, 70 x 59 inches, cotton, pieced. Purchase. Collection of Old State
House Museum. 88.40.1.

Plate 46. Buzz Saw Quilt, made by Docella Johnson, Bradley, Arkansas, circa 1900–1920, 79 x 76 1/2 inches, cotton, pieced. Purchase. Collection of Old State House Museum. 88.42.1.

Plate 47. Rising Sun Quilt, made by Beulah Smith, Paragould, Arkansas, 1924, 80 x 70 inches, cotton, piecd. Purchase. Collection of Old State House Museum. 88.42.2.

Plate 48. Rising Sun, a detail.

The Quilts

Plate 49. Nursery Rhyme Quilt, made by Dorothy Lambert White, Conway, Arkansas, circa 1940, 78 x 66 inches, cotton, embroidered. A child's quilt made from a mail-order iron-on transfer pattern. Gift of Malsie A. Osborne, Conway, Arkansas. Collection of Old State House Museum. 90.25.4.

Plate 50. Strip Quilt, made by Dorothy Lambert White, Conway, Arkansas, circa 1940, 86 x 60 inches, cotton, pieced. Gift of Malsie A. Osborne, Conway, Arkansas. Collection of Old State House Museum. 90.25.1.

Plate 51. Broken Dishes Quilt, made by Dorothy Lambert White, circa 1950, 77 x
61 1/2 inches, cotton, pieced. Gift of Malsie A. Osborne, Conway, Arkansas.
Collection of Old State House Museum. 90.25.3.

Plate 52. Fly Foot and Nine Patch Quilt, made by Dorothy Lambert White, Conway, Arkansas, circa 1940, 76 1/2 x 63 1/2 inches, cotton, pieced. Gift of Malsie A. Osborne, Conway, Arkansas. Collection of Old State House Museum. 90.25.2.

Plate 53. Friendship Star Quilt, made by Dorothy Lambert White, Conway,
Arkansas, circa 1940, 89 x 60 inches, cotton, pieced. Gift of Malsie A. Osborne,
Conway, Arkansas. Collection of Old State House Museum. 90.25.5.

Plate 54. Star of Bethlehem Quilt, made by Leonia Taylor, Arkansas, circa 1900, cotton, pieced. Purchase. Collection of Old State House Museum. 96.01.8.

Plate 55. Four Patch Quilt, made by Leonia Taylor, Arkansas, circa 1920, cotton,
pieced. Purchase. Collection of Old State House Museum. 96.01.9.

Plate 56. Spools Quilt, made by Leonia Taylor, Arkansas, no date, cotton, pieced.
Purchase. Collection of Old State House Museum. 96.01.11.

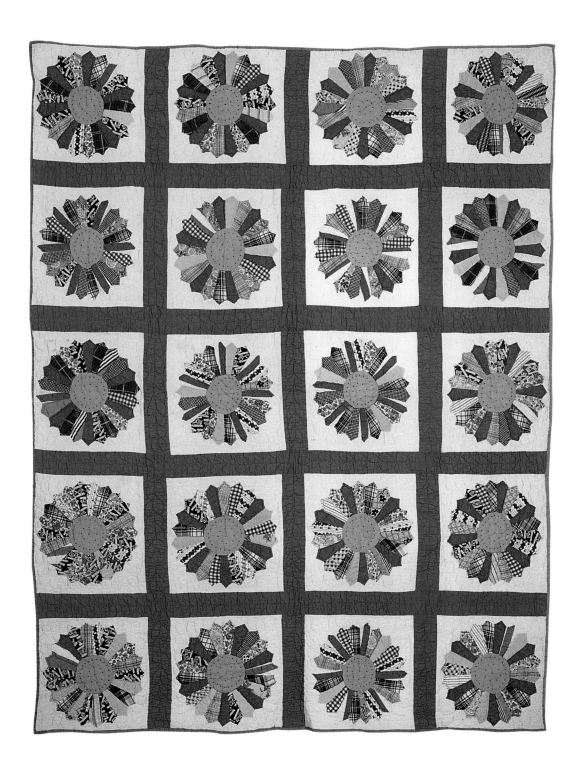

Plate 57. Fancy Dresden Plate Quilt, made by Leonia Taylor, Arkansas, circa 1920–1930, cotton, pieced. Purchase. Collection of Old State House Museum. 96.01.10.

Plate 58. Contained Crazy Quilt, made by Lula Bradford James, Dodderidge, Arkansas, circa 1950, silk, satin pieced. Collection of Old State House Museum. 97.01.3.

Plate 59. Flower Basket Quilt, made by Lula Bradford James, Dodderidge,
Arkansas, circa 1930. Unusual use of ruching on the quilt. Purchase. Collection of
Old State House Museum. 97.01.4.

Plate 60. Salesman Sample Quilt, made by Lula Bradford James, Dodderidge, Arkansas, circa 1940–1950, suitings materials, pieced. Purchase. Collection of Old State House Museum. 97.01.6.

Plate 61. Broken Star with Zigzag Border, made by Lula Bradford James,
Dodderidge, Arkansas, circa 1930, not quilted until 1980, cotton, pieced. Purchase.
Collection of Old State House Museum. 97.01.5.

Plate 62. Donkey Quilt or Giddap, A Very Democratic Donkey Quilt, made by
Beatrice Ruth Calhoun Williamson, Texarkana, Arkansas, 1932–1934, cotton,
pieced. Purchase. Collection of Old State House Museum. 96.01.17.

The Quilts

Plate 63. Strip Quilt, made by Jessie Jones, Crossett, Arkansas, circa 1960, 89 1/2 x
81 inches, coton, polyester, tacked, not quilted, pieced. Gift of Sandra Todaro,
Shreveport, Louisiana. Collection of Old State House Museum. 89.36.

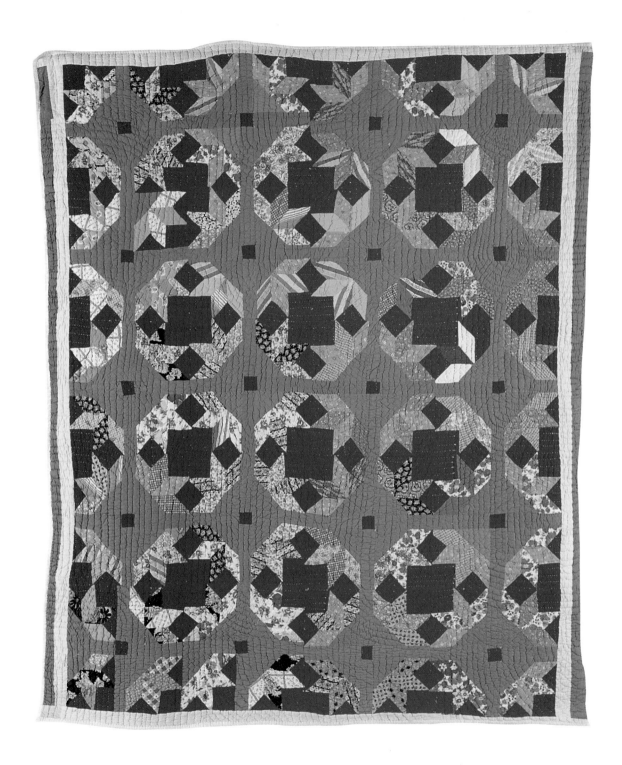

Plate 64. Turkey Tracks Variation Quilt, made by Sally Epps, Taylor, Arkansas, late 1930s, 79 x 63 1/2 inches, cotton, pieced. Purchase. Collection of Old State House Museum. 90.26.

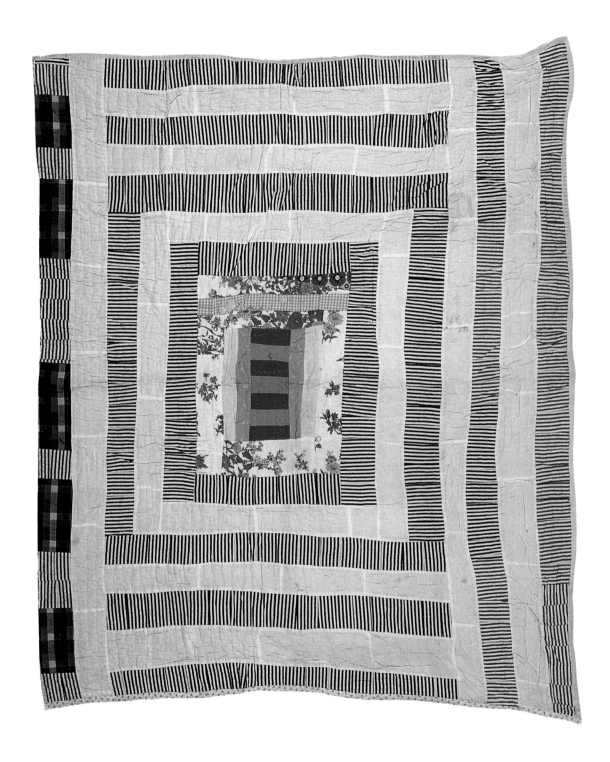

Plate 65. Medallion Quilt, made by Dallie Head, Dodderidge, Arkansas, circa 1940, 73 1/2 x 63 1/4 inches, cotton, pieced. Purchase. Collection of Old State House Museum. 91.08.1.

Plate 66. Log Cabin Quilt, made by Jessie Lee Jones, Shreveport, Louisiana, 1967, 87 x 68 inches, cotton, polyester, taffeta, pieced. Collection of Old State House Museum. 90.29.

The Quilts

Plate 67. Quilt name unknown, made by Mae Thompson, Arkansas, cotton, pieced. Purchase. Collection of Old State House Museum. 96.08.

Plate 68. Nine Patch and Rolling Stone Quilt, maker unknown, Little Rock, Arkansas, circa 1930, cotton, pieced. Purchase. Collection of Old State House Museum. 89.08.

Plate 69. Central Medallion Quilt, maker unknown, Cotton Plant, Arkansas, circa 1970, 76 1/2 x 69 inches, polyester satin, ribbon material, pieced. Reported to be a funeral cover. Purchase. Collection of Old State House Museum. 95.14.1.

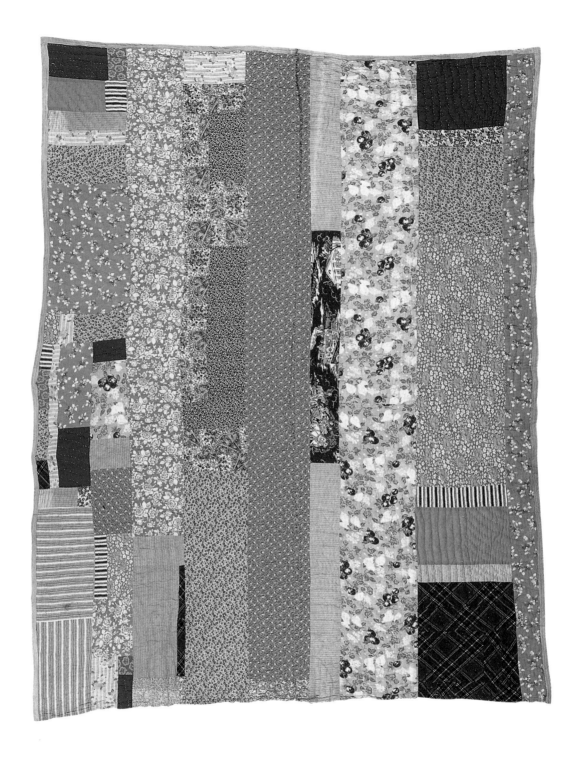

Plate 70. Strip Quilt, maker unknown, Cotton Plant, Arkansas, circa 1920–1930, 83 1/2 x 66 inches, cotton, home-dyed feed-sack material, pieced. Purchase. Collection of Old State House Museum. 95.14.3.

Plate 71. Double Pyramid Quilt, maker unknown, Cotton Plant, Arkansas, circa 1950, 70 1/2 x 68 1/4 inches, cotton, pieced. Purchase. Collection of Old State House Museum. 95.14.4.

Plate 72. String Diamonds Quilt, maker unknown, circa 1920–1930, 76 x 61 1/2 inches, machine pieced and quilted. Purchase. Collection of Old State House Museum. 95.14.2.

Plate 73. Miniature Churn Dash Quilt, made by Gloria Scott, Hot Springs, Arkansas, circa 1980, cotton, pieced. Gift of Sandra and Joe Todaro, Shreveport, Louisiana. Collection of Old State House Museum. 96.12.7.

Plate 74. Miniature Grandmother's Fan Quilt, made by Gloria Scott, Hot Springs, Arkansas, circa 1980, cotton, pieced. Gift of Sandra and Joe Todaro, Shreveport, Louisiana. Collection of Old State House Museum. 96.12.4.

Plate 75. Miniature Four Patch of Hearts Quilt, made by Gloria Scott, Hot Springs, Arkansas, circa 1980, cotton, pieced. Gift of Sandra and Joe Todaro, Shreveport, Louisiana. Collection of Old State House Museum. 96.12.1.

Plate 76. Miniature Diamond in a Square Quilt, made by Gloria Scott, Hot Springs, Arkansas, circa 1980, cotton, pieced. Gift of Sandra and Joe Todaro, Shreveport, Louisiana. Collection of Old State House Museum. 96.12.2.

Plate 77. Miniature Roman Stripes Quilt, made by Gloria Scott, Hot Springs,
Arkansas, circa 1980, cotton, pieced. Gift of Sandra and Joe Todaro, Shreveport,
Louisiana. Collection of Old State House Museum. 96.12.3.

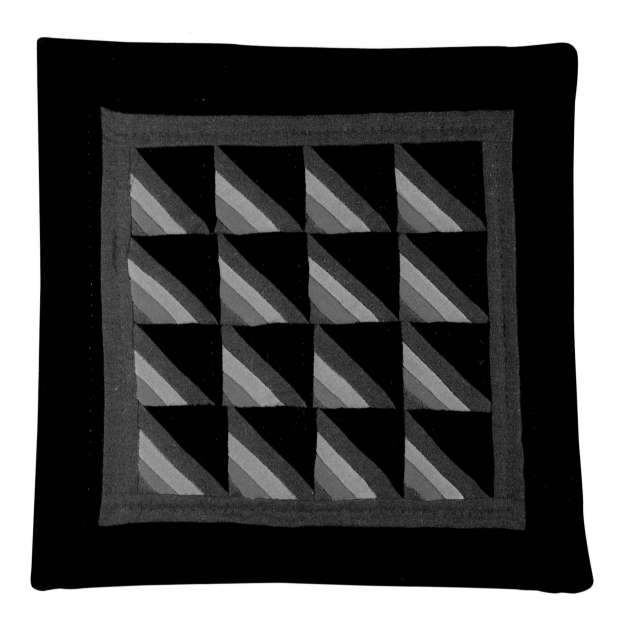

Plate 78. Miniature Bars Quilt, made by Gloria Scott, Hot Springs, Arkansas, cotton, pieced. Gift of Sandra and Joe Todaro, Shreveport, Louisiana. Collection of Old State House Museum. 96.12.5.

Plate 79. Miniature Irish Chain Quilt, made by Gloria Scott, Hot Springs,
Arkansas, circa 1980, cotton, pieced. Gift of Sandra and Joe Todaro, Shreveport,
Louisiana. Collection of Old State House Museum. 96.12.6.

Appendix 1

Tabulation of Number of Black-made Quilts by Date in the Collection

1890/1900s	1910s	1920s	1930s	1940s	1950s
3		9	16	18	9

1960s	1970s	1980s	1990s
4	6	10	1

Demographic Distribution of Black Quiltmaking Population Represented in the Old State House Museum's Quilt Collection

The majority of the quilts in the Old State House Museum's collection were made by black Arkansans who lived in rural areas in the southern half of the state. Little Rock, Helena, and Pine Bluff were Arkansas urban centers where most black city dwellers settled. Only Little Rock is represented by a quilt in the collection; the other urban centers are not.

Quiltmaking Techniques Preferred by Black Arkansans as Indicated by the Percentages Employed

93 percent pieced; 4 percent pieced and appliquéd; 1 percent embroidered; 1 percent appliquéd; 1 percent novelty (yo-yo).

Black Arkansan Families and the Number of Their Quilts in the Museum Collection

Allen/Williams Family, Camden, Arkansas

Mary Ann Allen, mother: 0
    Cordelia Allen Green, daughter: 2
    Mary Allen Smith Williams, daughter: 9
        Tillie Rae Williams Hall, granddaughter: 3
        Hattie Williams Jones, granddaughter: 7

Wilson Family, Calion, Arkansas

Frances Smith Wilson, mother: 1
    Authorine Wilson Anderson, daughter: 1
    Eldora Wilson Thomas, daughter: 1
    Minnie Ola Wilson Leary, daughter: 1
    Welthia Wilson Wardlaw, daughter: 1

Collins/Wilson Family, Magnolia, Arkansas

Hattie Collins, mother: 1
    Lucy Collins Wilson, daughter: 0
        Herma Wilson Williams, granddaughter: 3
        Essie Jackson, granddaughter (cousin to Herma, not sister): 2

Parker/Hall Family, Emerson, Arkansas

Sally Anna Ingram Parker, mother: 1
    Catherine Parker Hall, daughter: 1
    Oscar Evans, cousin by marriage: 1

Shed/Bennett Family, Camden, Arkansas

Asia Cummings Shed, mother: 2
    Malsie Shed Bennett, daughter: 3
        Myrtle Bennett, granddaughter: 1

Appendix 2

Names found for unusual quilt with folded triangles sewn down on one side only, then placed in concentric circles onto a backing: Pine Cone, Pine Burr, Target, Bull's Eye, Cockleburr, Quill, Prairie Points, Prairie Points in a Circle, Sunburst variation.

Black-made Pine Cone quilts have been found in Arkansas, Florida, Tennessee, Alabama, Kentucky, Mississippi, Georgia, North Carolina. Recorded versions of Pine Cone quilts include ones made by the following quilters:

Mary Allen Smith Williams, Arkansas
Oscar Evans, Arkansas
Catherine Parker Hall, Arkansas
China Grove Myles, Alabama
Lucy Marie Mingo, Alabama
Maker's name unknown, Alabama (quilt now in Oberlin, Ohio)
Hattie McWilliams, Kentucky
Frances S. Chapman, Georgia
Rebecca ("Becky") Rascoe, North Carolina
Addie Bullock, Florida
Ozella Angel, Tennessee
Maker's name unknown, Tennessee (quilt now in Evansville, Indiana)
Maker's name unknown, quilt in collection of Fisk University, Nashville,
     Tennessee
Sadie Blackburn, Mississippi

Documented white-made versions of Pine Cone quilts have been found in Texas, Oklahoma, Georgia, North Carolina, and Ohio.

PINE BURR, PINE CONE QUILT ANNOTATED REFERENCES

America's Quilts and Coverlets by Safford and Bishop. New York: E. P. Dutton, 1972. Fig. 223 (left). Appliqué Sunburst variation, circa 1850. "to make 'petals' that are raised above the surface of the spread."

Antique Gazette. February 1988, p. 3A. "Middle Tennessee Historic Homes Celebrate Black History," picture with caption, "An Oakland volunteer examines a quilt made by a black crafts person" (no name of quilt given).

Antique Monthly. September 1975, p. 10B. "Variation of the Sunburst Pattern, Southern," circa 1850, same quilt as shown in Safford and Bishop.

Design and Content: The Artistry of Antique American Quilts. 21 April–16 May 1996. The Gallery at Bristol-Myers Squibb, Princeton, New Jersey, exhibition catalog, p. 8. Target (also called Prairie Points or Pine Burr) pieced quilt, cotton, circa 1880, found in North Carolina, p. 10, catalog text, re: quilt. (Quilt sold by Laura Fisher Antiques.)

Florida Quilts by Charlotte Williams. Gainesville: University Press of Florida, 1992. Plate 94, Pine Cone. Made by Addie Bullock in Marianna, Florida, in 1966. Dimensions 63 x 86 inches cotton top; sewn by hand, quilted by hand; no batting, striped cotton backing, illus. p. 158, text p. 155.

The Freedom Quilting Bee by Nancy Callahan. Tuscaloosa: University of Alabama Press, 1987. Plate 8 (color), opposite p. 117. China Grove Myles's Pine Burr quilt, p. 176. China Grove Myles, a few months before her death in 1976 (Pine Burr quilt in the background), p. 183. Lucy Marie Mingo "continues the Pine Burr tradition of China Grove Myles, her aunt by marriage. Quilt has 23,850 pieces."

Lone Stars: A Legacy of Texas Quilts, 1836–1936 by Karoline Patterson and Nancy O'Bryant Puentes. Austin: University of Texas Press, 1986, pp. 126–27. "Target Quilt, circa 1910, made by Lorah Sasser Clark in Nancy Prairie, or Whitesboro, Grayson County" (mentions a quilt of similar construction found in New Mexico, known as "Pequito quilt").

The Magazine Antiques, September 1988. Laura Fisher adv. Target pattern pieced quilt. Afro-American, circa 1940, Southern.

North Carolina Quilts by Ruth Haislip Roberson, et al. Chapel Hill: University of North Carolina Press with the North Carolina Quilt Project, 1988. Plates 4–25, p. 126. Pine Cone, 1920s Bertie County by Rebecca (Becky) Rascoe. 63 x 72 inches. Owned by Lucy Rascoe Outlaw Gillam. Text p. 125. Becky Rascoe was an African American.

Oklahoma Heritage Quilts: A Sampling of Quilts Made in or Brought to Oklahoma before 1940. Oklahoma Heritage Project. Paducah, KY: American Quilter's Society, 1990, p. 51. Prairie Points in a Circle (Target or Quill) made by Ora Robertson Baughier (1880–1949). Made in Decatur, Texas, early 1900s.

Quilt Digest #4. Michael Kile, ed. San Francisco: Quilt Digest Press, 1986, p. 43. Quilt made by Lorah Sasser Clark, Grayson County, Texas, circa 1910, p. 25. "Helping People to Help Themselves," by Nancy Callahan. Pine Burr by Lucy Marie Mingo, Gees Bend, Alabama, caption: "Mrs. Mingo's aunt by marriage, China Grove Myles, developed the elaborate piecing technique employed in the Pine Burr design." Collection of the quiltmaker.

Quilts of Illusion by Laura Fisher. Pittstown, NJ: Main Street Press, 1988, p. 117; fig. 3.112. Target Quilt (Quill variation), circa 1930. Made by Hattie McWilliams, Kentucky, a black quilter.

SITELINE. January 1980. S.I.T.E.S. (Smithsonian Institution Traveling Exhibitions Service). "Contemporary Afro-American Quilts," exhibition of thirty quilts. Organized by Maude Wahlman of Yale University. Pine Cone quilt by Sadie Blackburn from *Contemporary Afro-American Quilts.*

Notes

Tracing the Line

1. Louise Gordon, *The Black Experience in Arkansas, 1880–1920* (Ph. D. dissertation, University of Arkansas, 1989).

2. Tom Baskett Jr., *Persistence of the Spirit: The Black Experience in Arkansas* (Little Rock: Resource Center, Arkansas Endowment for the Humanities, 1986), p. 4.

3. Marianne Woods, *Stitches in Time: A Legacy of Ozark Quilts* (Rogers, AR: Rogers Historical Museum, 1986), pp. 35–36.

4. Jan Tyler, "Folks Warm Up to Arkansas Country Quilts," in *Rural Arkansas* (November 1988), pp. 4–5, 8.

5. Roland L. Freeman, *A Communion of the Spirits: African American Quilters, Preservers, and Their Stories* (Nashville, TN: Rutledge Hill Press, 1996), pp. 203–7.

6. James S. Griffith, *Geometry in Motion: Afro-American Quiltmakers of Pinal County, Arizona* (Tucson: Southwest Folklore Center, University of Arizona, 1981). Judy Hille, "In Stitches: Display Covers the Afro-American Influences on Quilting," *Arizona Republic* (April 4, 1981).

7. Marsha MacDowell and Ruth Fitzgerald, eds., *Michigan Quilts: 150 Years of a Textile Tradition* (East Lansing: Michigan State University Museum, 1987), p. 103, fig. 154. Marsha MacDowell, ed., *African American Quiltmaking in Michigan* (East Lansing: Michigan State University Press in collaboration with the Michigan State University Museum), p. 65, fig. 99.

8. MacDowell and Fitzgerald, *Michigan Quilts,* p. 70, fig. 94. MacDowell, *African American Quiltmaking in Michigan,* p. 57, fig. 86.

9. MacDowell, *African American Quiltmaking in Michigan,* p. 64, fig. 98.

10. Gladys-Marie Fry, *Broken Star: Post–Civil War Quilts Made by Black Women* (Dallas, TX: Museum of African American Life and Culture, 1986), p. 9, fig. 10, and p. 12. In an interview with Alice Trammell's granddaughter, Alfreda Cole of Muskegon, Michigan, Gladys-Marie Fry learned that the former slave, Alice Trammell, was taught to sew when living as a house servant on a plantation in Arkansas. As an adult she became a midwife, living her entire life in the Magnolia area. MacDowell, *African American Quiltmaking in Michigan,* p. 64, fig. 98.

11. Eli Leon, *Who'd a Thought It: Improvisation in African American Quiltmaking* (San Francisco, CA: San Francisco Craft and Folk Art Museum,

1987), p. 36, fig. 15. Double Wedding Ring quilt made in Sweet Home, Arkansas, circa 1940, by Emma Hall. It's a highly unusual adaptation of the traditional Double Wedding Ring and appears to be a combination of a fan pattern and a wedding ring pattern.

12. Baskett, *Persistence of the Spirit,* p. 35.

13. Cuesta Benberry, *Always There: The African American Presence in American Quilts* (Louisville: Kentucky Quilt Project, 1992), pp. 51–56. "The Perkins Family Quilts" relates a story spanning one hundred years of a close-knit, multigenerational black family's quiltmaking. Beginning in nineteenth-century Virginia, the account traces the Perkins family's quiltmaking activities at the homestead and of younger generations who migrated to West Virginia, to Philadelphia, and to New York City, while still maintaining the family quilting tradition.

ARKANSAS'S BLACK QUILTMAKERS AND THEIR QUILTS

1. Telephone interview of Kathlyn Sullivan by author, October 1, 1998. In our small sample (not definitive by any means) of Pine Cone/Pine Burr/Target quilts, the white-made ones ranged in dates from circa 1850–1920s; the black-made examples were dated circa 1920–1970s. Allowing for any misdating, it does appear black quilters did continue to make Pine Cone quilts until the latter part of the twentieth century.

2. Nancy Callahan, *The Freedom Quilting Bee* (Tuscaloosa: University of Alabama Press, 1987), pp. 175–81. Callahan tells of the life of legendary Alabama maker of Pine Burr quilts, China Grove Myles, and how she became famous for making this kind of quilt. Bets Ramsey and Merikay Waldvogel, *Quilts of Tennessee: Images of Domestic Life Prior to 1930* (Nashville, TN: Rutledge Hill Press, 1987), p. 76. Ozella Angel, a black quilter from Chattanooga, recalls making this type of quilt which she called "Cockleburr." (not illustrated).

3. Kathlyn Sullivan, "Pieced and Plentiful," in *North Carolina Quilts* (Chapel Hill, NC: University of North Carolina Press and the North Carolina Quilt Project, 1988), pp. 124–26. Rebecca ("Becky") Rascoe of the Indian Woods Community in Bertie County, North Carolina, a black quilter, made a Pine Cone doll quilt for the young white daughter, Lucy Rascoe Outlaw Gilliam, of the owner of the farm on which Becky worked.

4. Maude Wahlman, *Signs and Symbols: African Images in African American Quilts* (New York: Studio Books in association with the Museum of American Folk Art, 1993), p. 47. African American doll quilt from North Carolina, maker unidentified.

5. Wilene Smith, *Quilt Patterns: An Index to the Kansas City Star Patterns 1928–1961* (Wichita, KS: self-published, 1985), p. 10. Louise O. Townsend, "Kansas City Star Quilt Patterns: 1928–1949," in *Uncoverings 1984: The Research Papers of the American Quilt Group,* Vol. 5, Sally Garoutte, ed. (Mill

Valley, CA: AQSG, 1985), p. 115. The Arkansas Snowflake quilt pattern was published in the *Kansas City* newspaper, February 9, 1935. It appeared also in the *Weekly Kansas City Star,* February 13, 1935. As the weekly edition of this newspaper did circulate in Arkansas, this pattern of the Arkansas Snowflake may have served as the model for Hattie Williams Jones's adaptation, the Snowflake quilt. She reported that some of her quilt patterns came from newspapers.

6. An interview of Malverna Richardson, St. Louis, Missouri, by author, August 1978. Malverna Richardson was born in Smithville, Mississippi, in 1923. She was taught to make quilts by her mother and completed her first quilt when she was ten years old. In their family they had three types of quilts: one for cover sleeping; a bedspread type to go on top, mostly used when company came; and a third type for being sick. When her family moved to St. Louis from Mississippi traveling on a train, she wrapped her children in the first string quilt she remembered making. In 1982 she was designated "Master Quilter" by the Missouri State Arts Council and was paid to teach quiltmaking to apprentices.

7. Sandra Todaro's field notes to the Old State House Museum of an interview with Eldora Wilson Thomas, June 25, 1996.

8. Sandra Todaro's field notes to Old State House Museum of an interview with Herma Wilson Williams, April 11, 1988.

9. Laura Fisher, *Quilts of Illusion* (Pittstown, NJ: Main Street Press, 1988), p. 117, fig. 3.112. Target Quilt (Quill variation). Charlotte Allen Williams, *Florida Quilts* (Gainesville: University Press of Florida, 1992), pp. 155, 158. Pine Cone quilt made by Addie Bullock, a black quilter, in Marianna, Florida, in 1966. Unpublished black-made versions of Pine Cone quilts brought to my attention: a six-block Pine Cone, predominently blue prints from Tennessee, dated circa 1920. (Refer to Katy Christopherson, Louisville, Kentucky.) Pine Cone quilt in a block configuration in the Fisk University, Nashville, Tennessee, collection, shown at Hunter Museum, Chattanooga, Tennessee, exhibition. (Refer to Bets Ramsey, Nashville, Tennessee.) Pine Cone quilt in all-over series of rows of concentric circles, made in Alabama, first two decades of the twentieth century (brought to Ricky Clark's 1983 FAVA exhibition "Quilts and Carousels: Folk Art in the Firelands").

10. Fisher, *Quilts of Illusion,* p. 111.

11. Ruby S. McKim, *Designs Worth Doing, 1931–32* (Independence, MO: McKim Studio, 1932). (a needlework catalog series, including quilts; published annually).

12. Dolores A. Hinson, *Quilting Manual* (New York: Hearthside Press, 1966), p. 156. Listing popular quilt patterns of the 1930s, Dolores Hinson cited Butterflys, Sunbonnet Sue, Overhaul Sam, Sailboats.

13. Barbara Brackman, *Clues in the Calico: A Guide to Identifying and Dating Antique Quilts* (McLean, VA: EPM Pub., 1989), pp. 143–45.

14. Joyce Gross and Cuesta Benberry, *Twentieth-Century Quilts: Women*

Make Their Mark (Paducah, KY: American Quilter's Society, 1997), p. 10. "Including men's neckties in such a way that they are easily recognized as being neckties by their shapes may be a 20th century innovation."

    15. "Giddap, A Very Democratic Donkey," by Eveline Foland, *The Kansas City Star,* July 22, 1931.

    16. Miniature quilts.

    17. Elaine Hedges, "The Nineteenth-Century Diarist and Her Quilts," in *Feminist Studies,* 8 (Summer 1982).

Glossary

album quilt. Quilt in which each block is of a different design, often made and signed by a different person.

appliqué. A process whereby small cut-out fabric pieces are laid on top of a base fabric and sewn down to form a design.

backing. The bottom fabric layer of a three-layered quilt; also called the lining.

batting. The middle layer of a three-layered quilt, usually of soft cotton, wool, or polyester. It is the inner or filler layer that provides warmth.

block. The basic geometric unit (a square, rectangle, triangle) of a patchwork quilt top; may be pieced, appliquéd, or embroidered. A number of blocks are sewn together to form the whole quilt top.

crazy quilt. A pieced or appliquéd free-form quilt of randomly shaped pieces sewn to a base. Nineteenth-century silk and velvet crazy quilts were frequently embellished with contrasting embroidered seams. Black-made rural Akansas crazy quilts were most often made of wool or cotton pieces without heavily embroidered seams.

cut by eye. A practice of many rural black Arkansans to cut directly into the cloth without the use of guiding templates for their patterns. They used only their eyes to judge the measurements of a block or a patch.

domestic cloth. A term used by nineteenth-century and early twentieth-century Americans to mean unbleached muslin fabric.

feed-sack material. Large quantities of staples, such as flour, sugar, and feed for farm animals came packaged in fabric bags. The fabric bags, when emptied, were utilized for making quilts, clothing, and various household needs.

improvisational piecing. A process whereby the quilter ignores standard traditional quiltmaking conventions and instead produces a spontaneous "inventive design-as you-go" quilt. Influenced by factors such as the limited amount of scrap materials available to her, the purpose of quickly constructing a ultilitarian quilt, and her creative mind-set, the quilter is little concerned with matching block corners or of establishing with regularity a single design element to move across the quilt. Many impoverished southern rural black quilters are especially noted for making improvisationally pieced quilts. Some southern rural white women of the same economic class have also made this type of quilt. Improvisationally pieced quilts differ so radically in appearance from traditional American patchwork quilts, they are today recognized as a form of folk art.

Lazy Gal quilt. An informally and quickly put together strip quilt often made by southern rural black quiltmakers.

Log Cabin quilt. One of the most popular of the pieced patterns in America. It is pieced in strips to form blocks and is subject to endless arrangements of the light and dark strips. The different arrangements of the blocks are assigned names; some of the most well known are Court House Steps, Pineapple, White House Steps, Barn Raising, and Log Cabin.

medallion quilt. A central panel is the focus of the quilt, and the panel is surrounded by borders. This is a very old configuration used as far back as the eighteenth century as a quilt design in Europe and America.

nine-patch quilt. Nine small squares sewn together in three rows to make one quilt block; often used as the first quilt block design taught to young children who are beginners at quiltmaking.

one-patch quilt. Quilt contains many pieces of one basic same-sized square, triangle, rectangle, hexagon, or diamond. When all of the like pieces are sewn together, in an arrangement of the maker's choosing, it becomes the quilt top.

pieced quilt. Sometimes called patchwork quilt and is the most popular type of quilt made in America. Small pieces of fabric are sewn together very often in a block arrangement, then a number of the blocks are sewn together to form the quilt top.

Pine Burr quilt. Also called Pine Cone, Bull's Eye, Target. Small squares are folded into triangles, then sewn to a background fabric on one side only, leaving the point of the triangle free. The triangles are sewn in ever-widening concentric circles, so the finished product looks like rings and rings of three-dimensional little points of fabric. Pine Burr quilts were much favored by southern rural black quilters.

prairie points. A name given to the tiny squares folded into triangles and used to make Pine Burr quilts. Many midwestern white quilters used prairie points to provide a decorative edging to their quilts.

quilt. A three-layered fabric sandwich, consisting of a decorated top layer, a middle or interlining layer of a soft material like cotton or wool, and a bottom layer, called the backing or lining. The three layers are held together by quilting stitches.

quilting horses. In rural communities the side rails or poles of the quilting frame needed to hold the fabric sandwich taut, were often placed over the backs of chairs, as the quilters often did not own a standing quilting frame. The quilting poles without a stand were called "quilting horses."

quilt kit. A commercially prepared package or box containing the "makings" of a quilt, which that quiltmaker then sews together. For a pieced kit, the patches are usually die-cut to be of uniform size and shape. For an appliqué quilt kit, stamped background material is provided and the various small patches to be laid onto the background and sewn down are included. For an embroidered quilt kit, the purchaser is given stamped background material to guide the maker in embroidering in cross-stitch, outline embroidery, or crewel embroidery. At times the embroidery thread is enclosed as part of the kit. Other times, the embroidery thread is a separate purchase and may be relatively expensive, costing as much or even more than the quilt kit. Quilt kits have been advertised as relieving the quiltmakers of the chore of cutting so much fabric necessary for constructing a quilt. Opponents of quilt kits compare them to cake mixes, to other prepared convenience foods, and paint-by-number art.

quilting stitch. The stitching that is used to fasten the three layers of the fabric sandwich—the quilt—together.

recovered quilt. An example of early recycling. When a quilt became too tattered for use, it was seldom discarded by poor people in rural areas. The old quilt was used as the batting or middle layer, and a new top and lining were placed over it.

regional quilt pattern names. With the advent of the publication of quilt pattern names in the nineteenth century and to a greater extent in the twentieth century, the names of the traditional quilt designs became somewhat standardized nationwide. Yet in certain regions of the country quilt names continued to vary from the norm and were often idiosyncratic to a particular area. Instances of regional pattern naming that coincided with their farm backgrounds were found among the rural black quilters of Arkansas. They called a trilobed leaf motif "chicken feet."

strip quilt. Long strips of cloth were either cut or torn and seamed together, placed vertically or horizontally. It was a fairly easy and quick quilt construction, as the maker had to sew only straight seams. Many southern black quiltmakers favored this type of quilt.

summer quilt. A two-layered quilt, without the middle batting layer. It was also called a coverlet, or a bedspread, and was used in warm weather.

template. A pattern shape made of a hard substance, such as tin, cardboard, or plastic that would not bend out of shape quickly, as it was used to trace the shape onto the fabric by drawing around it.

tied quilt. When yarn or a strong twine thread, placed at strategic intervals, is used to fasten the quilt's three layers together instead of using the thread for a continuous quilting stitch, it is called a tied quilt.

whole cloth quilt. An all-quilted work, with no decorated top of appliqué, piecework, or embroidery. Placed on a plain-colored fabric top, the quilting itself forms the decoration. Whole cloth quiltmaking was greatly favored in Europe, both in the early centuries and in recent times.

yo-yo quilt. A novelty work but as it is not quilted, it is not actually a quilt. Small circles of fabric are cut, and a thread is run around the edge, then pulled up tightly. The circle is thus doubled. Each circle is sewn to the next circle about halfway down the sides, until enough yo-yos are joined to make a full top. A yo-yo top needs to be placed like a bedspread over a plain-colored sheet, as the holes at the sides of the yo-yos give it a somewhat lacy, see-through look. Yo-yos were in vogue during the first three decades of the twentieth century and enjoyed a multitude of uses for quiltmaking and for clothing.

Selected Bibliography

A Pattern Book: Based on an Appliqué Quilt by Mrs. Harriet Powers American, Nineteenth Century. Boston: Museum of Fine Arts, nd.

Arkansas Quilter's Guild. *Arkansas Quilts.* Paducah, KY: American Quilter's Society, 1987.

Arkansas: Year of American Craft, 1993. Little Rock: Arkansas Arts Center Decorative Arts Museum, 1993.

Baskett, Tom, ed. *Persistence of the Spirit: The Black Experience in Arkansas.* Little Rock: Arkansas Endowment for the Humanities, 1986.

Bell, Michael, and Carole Bell. *Quilting: Folk Traditions of the Rhode Island Afro-American Community.* Providence, RI: Black Heritage Society. nd.

Benberry, Cuesta. *Always There: The African-American Presence in American Quilts.* Louisville: Kentucky Quilt Project, 1992.

———. "A Quilt Research Surprise." *Quilter's Newsletter Magazine* (July/August 1981), pp. 34–35. Research revealed the existence of a quilt made in 1836 for an antislavery fair, held in Boston. Quilt, inscribed with a poignant poem telling of slave mother's plight, now housed at the Society for the Preservation of New England Antiquities, Harrison-Grey-Otis House, Boston.

———. "White Perceptions of Blacks in Quilts and Related Media." *Uncoverings 1983: The Research Papers of the American Quilt Study Group.* ed. Sally Garoutte. Mill Valley, CA.: American Quilt Study Group, 1984. pp. 59–74. Research traces how black people were portrayed on quilts made by whites in America from the mid-1800s to the 1980s. Cited are the comic-derogatory stereotypical images of blacks so prevalent in the early years that gradually changed to more realistic portrayals, and the reasons for the changes.

———. "A Quilt for Queen Victoria." *Quilter's Newsletter Magazine.* (February 1987), pp. 24–25. Research revealed that a former American enslaved woman, Martha Ann Ricks, repatriated to Liberia, made a quilt for Queen Victoria, and traveled to England to present the quilt to the queen in 1892.

———. "Afro-American Slave Quilts and the British Connection." *America in Britain: Journal of the American Museum in Britain,* Bath, England, Vol. XXV Numbers 2 and 3. (Part 1, Fall 1987): (Part 2, Winter 1987). Research conducted primarily at the British Museum Library in London revealed the major role of English, Scottish, and Irish antislavery proponents in contributing liberally to the American abolitionist cause.

———. "A Style of Their Own: Two Black Quiltmakers." *American Quilter Magazine,* 4:1 (Spring 1988), pp. 20–25.

———. "The Story Tellers: African American Quilts Come to the Fore." *Quilter's Newsletter Magazine* (November 1990), pp. 46–47.

———. "Reflections on a Favorite Quilt: African Jazz in Black and White." *American Quilter Magazine* (Winter 1991), pp. 6–8.

———. "Always There: The African American Presence in American Quilts." *Quilter's Newsletter Magazine* (November 1991), pp. 42–45.

———, and Carol Crabb, eds. *A Patchwork of Pieces: An Anthology of Early Quilt Stories, 1845–1940.* Paducah, KY: American Quilter's Society, 1993. Quilt fiction.

———. "The Threads of African-American Quilters Are Woven into History," *American Visions: The Magazine of Afro-American Culture* (December/January 1994), pp. 14–18.

———. "African American Quilts: Paradigms of Black Diversity," *The International Review of African American Art* 12:3 (Winter 1995), pp. 4, 30–37.

Bennett, Swannee, and William B. Worthen. *Arkansas Made: A Survey of the Decorative, Mechanical, and Fine Arts Produced in Arkansas, 1819–1870.* Volume I. Fayetteville: University of Arkansas Press, 1990.

Benson, Jane, and Nancy Olson. *The Power of Cloth: Political Quilts, 1845–1986.* Cupertino, CA: Euphrat Gallery, 1987.

Brown, Barbara. "African American Quilts: What They Are, What They Are Not." *The Forty-third Washington Antiques Show.* Washington, DC, 1997. pp. 80–84.

Callahan, Nancy. *The Freedom Quilting Bee.* Tuscaloosa: University of Alabama Press, 1987.

Cameron, Dan, ed., et al. *Dancing at the Louvre: Faith Ringgold's French Collection and Other Story Quilts.* New York: New Museum of Contemporary Art, 1998.

Chase, Judith Wragg. *Afro-American Art and Craft.* New York: Van Nostrand Reinhold, 1971.

Chaveas, Lucille. "Who'd a Thought It: Improvisations in African American Quiltmaking." *Journal of American Folklore* (Fall 1992), pp. 477–79. Book review.

Chinn, Jennie A. "African American Quiltmaking Traditions: Some Assumptions Reviewed." *Kansas Quilts and Quilters.* Lawrence: University of Kansas Press, 1993. pp. 157–75.

Christopherson, Katy. *The Political and Campaign Quilt.* Frankfort: Kentucky Heritage Quilt Society, 1984.

Clark, Ricky. *Quilts and Carousels: Folk Art in the Firelands.* Oberlin, OH: Firelands Association for the Visual Arts, 1983.

———, et al. *Quilts in Community: Ohio's Traditions.* Nashville, TN: Rutledge Hill Press, 1991.

Cochran, Rachel, ed., et al. *New Jersey Quilts, 1777 to 1950: Contributions to an American Tradition.* Paducah, KY: American Quilters Society, 1992. "The African American Presence," pp. 146–49.

Dobard, Raymond G. "A Covenant in Cloth: The Visible and the Tangible in African American Quilts." *Connecting Stitches: Quilts in Illinois Life.* Springfield: Illinois State Museum, 1995. pp. 28–39.

———. "Quilts as Communal Emblems and Personal Icons." *International Review of African American Art,* 11:2 (1994), pp. 38–43.

Editorial Collective. *Star Quilt.* Bangalore, India: Streelekba, 1995.

Ferrero, Pat, Elaine Hedges, and Julie Silber. *Hearts and Hands: The Influence of Women and Quilts in American Society.* San Francisco: Quilt Digest Press, 1987.

Ferris, William, ed. *Afro-American Folk Arts and Crafts.* Boston: G. K. Hall, 1983.

Fisher, Laura. *Quilts of Illusion.* Pittstown, NJ: Main Street Press, 1988.

Flomenhaft, Eleanor. *Faith Ringgold: A Twenty-five Year Survey.* Hempstead, NY: Fine Arts Museum of Long Island, 1990.

Franger, Gaby, and Geetha Varadarajan, eds. *The Art of Survival: Fabric Images in Women's Daily Lives.* Nürnberg, Germany: Tara Pub., 1996.

Freeman, Roland. *Something to Keep You Warm: The Roland Freeman Collection of Black American Quilts from the Mississippi Heartland.* Jackson: Mississippi State Historical Museum, 1981.

———, and Rosemary Bray. "Keepsakes." *Essence Magazine* (November 1978), pp. 106–12.

———. *More Than Just Something to Keep You Warm: Tradition and Change in African American Quilting.* Philadelphia, PA: Springside School with Roland L. Freeman, 1992.

———. *A Communion of the Spirits: African American Quilters, Preservers, and Their Stories.* Nashville, TN: Rutledge Hill Press, 1996. Foreword by Cuesta Benberry.

Fry, Gladys-Marie. *Stitched from the Soul: Slave Quilts from the Ante-Bellum South.* New York: Dutton Studio Books with the Museum of American Folk Art, 1990.

———. *Broken Star: Post–Civil War Quilts Made by Black Women.* Dallas, TX: Museum of African American Life Culture, 1986.

———. *Man Made: African American Men and Quilting Traditions.* Washington, DC: Anacostia Museum and Center for African American History and Culture, 1998.

Glass, Barbara, ed. *Uncommon Beauty in Common Objects: The Legacy of African American Craft Art.* Wilberforce, OH: National Afro-American Museum and Cultural Center, 1993.

Gordon, Louise. *The Black Experience in Arkansas, 1880–1920.* Ph.D diss., Little Rock: University of Arkansas, 1989.

Griffith, James S. *Geometry in Motion: Afro-American Quiltmakers of Pinal*

County, Arizona. Tucson: Southwest Folklore Center, University of
    Arizona, 1981.

Grudin, Eva Ungar. *Stitching Memories: African American Story Quilts.*
    Williamstown, MA: Williams College Museum of Art, 1990.

Height, Dorothy, et al. *The Black Family Dinner Cookbook.* Washington, DC:
    National Council of Negro Women, 1993. Has illustrations of quilts by
    Michael Cummings, Carolyn Mazloomi, Sandra German, Marie
    Wilson, Anita Knox, Francelise Dawkins, and New York chapter of the
    Women of Color Quilters Network.

Hollander, Stacy. "African American Quilts: Two Perspectives." *Folk Art:
    Magazine of the Museum of American Folk Art* (Spring 1993), pp. 44–51.
    An account of two African American quilt exhibitions held simultane-
    ously at the Museum of American Folk Art, New York, *Signs and
    Symbols* curated by Maude Wahlman, and *Always There* curated by
    Cuesta Benberry.

Horton, Laurel, and Lynn R. Myers. *Social Fabric: South Carolina's Traditional
    Quilts.* Columbia: McKissick Museum, University of South Carolina.
    n.d. "Sea Island Black Quilters," by Nan Tournier, pp. 40–46.

Jeffries, Rosalind. "African Retentions in African American Quilts and
    Artifacts." *International Review of African American Art,* 11:2 (1994), pp.
    28–37.

Kusserow, Karl. "Threads of Evidence: Attributing an Anonymous Quilt to an
    African American Quiltmaker." *Folk Art* (Spring 1994), pp. 46–49.

Lamb, Venice, and Alastair Lamb. *West African Narrow Strip Weaving,* County
    Borough of Halifax. Canada: Halifax Museums, 1973.

Leon, Eli. *Who'd a Thought It: Improvisation in African-American Quiltmaking.*
    San Francisco: San Francisco Craft and Folk Art Museum, 1987.

———. *Models in the Mind: African Prototypes in American Patchwork.*
    Winston-Salem, NC: Diggs Gallery and Winston-Salem University,
    1992.

———. *Arbie Williams Transforms the Britches Quilt.* Regents of the University
    of California and Mary Porter Sesnon Art Gallery, 1993.

Livingston, Jane, and John Beardsley with Regenia Perry. *Black Folk Art in
    America, 1930–1980.* Corcoran Gallery, Washington, DC: University of
    Mississippi and the Center for the Study of Southern Culture, 1982.

Lohrenz, Mary Edna, and Anita Miller. *Mississippi Homespun: Nineteenth-
    Century Textiles and the Women Who Made Them.* Jackson: Mississippi
    Department of Archives and History, 1987.

MacDowell, Marsha L., ed. *African American Quiltmaking in Michigan.* East
    Lansing: Michigan State University Press, 1997.

———, and Ruth Fitzgerald, eds. *Michigan Quilts: 150 Years of a Textile
    Tradition.* East Lansing: Michigan State University Museum, 1987.

Mazloomi, Carolyn. *Spirits of the Cloth: Contemporary African American Quilts.*
    New York: Clarkson Potter, 1998. Preface by Faith Ringgold; Foreword
    by Cuesta Benberry.

McDonald, Mary Anne. "Jennie Burnett: Afro-American Quilter." *Five North Carolina Folk Artists*. Chapel Hill: Ackland Art Museum, 1986.

McKinney, Nancy, ed. *Traditions in Cloth: Afro-American Quilts/West African Textiles*. Los Angeles: California Afro-American Museum, 1986. Introduction by Cuesta Benberry.

McMorris, Penny. *Quilting II with Penny McMorris*. Bowling Green, OH: Bowling Green State University, 1982. Program Guidebook. Program 9: "Afro-American Quilts."

Needle, Cloth, and Time: A Celebration of Traditional Quiltmakers. Texarkana: Texarkana Regional Arts and Humanities Council, August 17–September 25, 1993. Exhibition catalog; Laurel Horton, guest curator.

Perry, Regenia. *Harriet Powers's Bible Quilts*. New York: Rizzoli International Pub., 1994.

Ramsey, Bets. *Quilt Close-Up: Five Southern Views*. Chattanooga, TN: Hunter Museum of Art, 1983.

Roberson, Ruth, ed. *North Carolina Quilts*. Chapel Hill: University of North Carolina Press, 1988.

Robinson, Charlotte, ed. *The Artist and the Quilt*. New York: Alfred A. Knopf, 1983.

Rogers Historical Museum. *Stitches in Time: A Legacy of Ozark Quilts*. Rogers, AR: 1986. pp. 35–36. Report of an African American quilting group in Fayetteville, Arkansas called "The Modern Priscillas," named for the early women's needlework magazine's title.

Roth, Moira. *Faith Ringgold: Change: Painted Story Quilts*. New York: Bernice Steinbaum Gallery, 1987.

Saint Louis Art Magazine. "New at the Museum: Jo Baker's Birthday" (March/April 1994), p. 8. Report of new quilt made by famous African American artist, Faith Ringgold, added to the museum collection. The quilt was commissioned by the St. Louis Art Museum in honor of Cuesta Benberry, who had curated the museum's first African American quilt exhibition the previous year.

Seiber, Roy. *African Textiles and Decorative Arts*. New York: Museum of Modern Art, 1973.

Smith Wilene. *Quilt Patterns: An Index to the Kansas City Star Patterns, 1928–1961*. Kechi, KS: Wilene Smith, 1985.

Thompson, Robert Farris. *Flash of the Spirit: African and Afro-American Art and Philosophy*. New York: Random House, 1981.

Tyler, Jan. "Folks Warm Up to Arkansas Country Quilts." *Rural Arkansas* (November 1988), pp. 4–8. About an Arkansas black quilt cottage industry formed by two quiltmaking sisters in Lexa, Arkansas.

Vlach, John Michael. *The Afro-American Tradition in Decorative Arts*. Cleveland, OH: Cleveland Museum of Art, 1978.

Wadsworth, Anna, ed. *Missing Pieces: Georgia Folk Art, 1770–1976*. Atlanta: Georgia Council for the Arts, 1976.

Wahlman, Maude S., and Ellen King Torrey. *Ten Afro-American Quilters.* University, MS: Center for the Study of Southern Culture, 1983.

———. *Signs and Symbols: African Images in African American Quilts.* New York: Studio Books in associaton with the Museum of American Folk Art, 1993.

Waldvogel, Merikay. *Soft Covers for Hard Times.* Nashville, TN: Rutledge Hill Press, 1990.

Master's thesis

Department of History, Applied History: Museum Studies McKissick Museum, University of South Carolina, Columbia. *Patchwork of Diversity: African American Quilts in the South Carolina Quilt Survey* by Carrie E. Taylor, 1995.

For Young Readers

Fedde, Gerry F. "The Quilt Craft of Harriet Powers." *Ebony Jr. Magazine* (March 1984), p. 13.

Flournoy, Valerie. *The Patchwork Quilt.* New York: Dial Books for Young Readers, E. P. Dutton, 1985.

Hopkinson, Deborah. *Sweet Clara and the Freedom Quilt.* New York: Alfred A. Knopf, 1995.

Lyons, Mary E. *Stitching Stars: The Story Quilts of Harriet Powers.* New York: Charles Scribners Sons for Young Readers, Macmillan, 1993.

Ringgold, Faith. *Tar Beach* New York: Crown, 1991. Caldecott medal awarded. The Faith Ringgold's books for young readers listed here are based on story quilts she made.

———. *Aunt Harriet's Underground Railroad in the Sky.* New York: Crown, 1992.

———. *Dinner at Aunt Connie's House.* New York: Hyperion Books for Children, 1993.

———. *Faith Ringgold's Talking Book.* New York: Crown Books for Young Readers, 1995.

Index